The Intuitive Wisdom of the Heart

A Collection of Poems of Encouragement

James P. Robson

HARDBACK: 978-1-947620-96-4
PAPERBACK: 978-1-947620-95-7
EBOOK: 978-1-947620-97-1

Ordering Information:

For orders and inquiries, please contact:
1-888-375-9818
www.toplinkpublishing.com
bookorder@toplinkpublishing.com

Printed in the United States of America

Contents

Introduction

This book is my eighth containing poems about life and also the various aspects of the human heart. The heart is misunderstood by many and yet is an intuitive and wisdom-based organ which functions as the chief administrator of mankind. Poetry is a method of communication with many various styles. The style I use is what I hear in my mind and is accentuated with both rhythm and rhyme. The style itself is only a format or a method of communicating ideas to enable the reader to understand the intended message.

Over many years, I have discovered and long believed that our primary purpose in life is to discover who we really are. We need to identify with ourselves and embark on a journey of self-discovery. As the question of who we are lingers and our curiosity continues to confront us, our need to answer this question intensifies. During my lifetime, I have learned much about the purpose and function of the human heart. Man's understanding of the heart is limited as the human heart accomplishes much more than what is obvious. Hopefully, many of my words will provide insight into both the heart and the mind and how they function in concert to fulfill God's will. The ideas inscribed in my many poems represent my determination and desire to connect with my Lord and

Savior Jesus Christ where I can find both rest and the knowledge of who I am. I believe that practice makes perfect and with patience and determination our search will lead to the treasure that confirms who we are and enables us to understand our Christian identity.

With much encouragement,

James P. Robson

Abiding Love

I came into this world
as a small and helpless child,
And soon after my birth
I was comforted and beguiled.

As I entered God's kingdom
in my mother's arms I was held,
She would nurture and embrace me
as her loving heart swelled.

My mother was my blessing
as I entered God's earth,
She guarded and protected
long before she gave birth.

My mother knew her purpose
and she knew just what to do,
She was focused on God's mission
and she would make sure that it came true.

Forever connected
my mother held me close,
Of all God's living persons
she loved me the most!

Adapting to Change

The earth and man's world
are at a crossroad of change,
The ways of the past are being discarded
so we must adapt and rearrange.

Rapid change is now upon us
we must accept and adapt,
Our solutions can be discovered
and our thinking must not react.

God created the heavens and the earth
to exist with continuous change,
With cycles repeating and man adjusting
to both the sunshine and the rain.

God's creative story
has activity clearly in mind,
So man can seek and discover
the treasure God intended for him to find.

The human mind seeks relaxation
and establishes habits that cannot be maintained,
As big changes take front and center
past thinking cannot be sustained.

Adaptation requires acceptance
and acceptance is essential for an exchange,
Release from your mind past thinking
and welcome in a new world of change!

Aligning Hearts and Minds

The earth is not my destination
it's not the place where I want to be,
I'm on a temporary assignment
in God's school of creative majesty.

He placed me here with a purpose
so I could freely seek out and find,
The secret to the mystery
of His creative and purely loving mind.

His mind is what I'm seeking
it's to what I intend to align,
In His image I was created
because I am the fruit of His blessed vine.

My time on earth is precious
and I must not waste a moment of my time,
I must focus and believe in His promise
our hearts beating in perfect rhythm and rhyme!

Answers to Prayer

Many are those who are seeking
for God to intervene in their affairs,
Without their concerns quickly answered
they conclude that He doesn't hear their prayers.

When we pray again and again
each time harder than the prayer before,
If the solutions aren't forthcoming
we stop praying and shut the door.

Are you really talking to the Father,
or are you talking to yourself alone?
Are you focusing on your problems,
or are you wanting to solve them on your own?

God is prepared to advise and answer
each and every request He receives,
Look for solutions and discover
as He sends answers to those who believe!

As Children

To enter the Kingdom of Heaven
you must come as if a child,
With purity and innocence
without thoughts that are defiled.

Jesus blessed the little children
and held them on His knee,
He showed them as He blessed them
for all the world to see.

Jesus loved the little children
just as His father taught Him to do,
A perfect union was established
making Heaven's sky the brightest blue.

Your heart and mind must work together
and focus clearly on God's plan,
Becoming childlike as Jesus taught us
to be like the great 'I Am"!

Ask

Ask, ask, ask
ask again, again. and again,
The Lord will hear you calling
He is the beginning and the end.

The Lord is always listening
He hears your every cry,
His mercy endures forever
both before and after you die.

Turn your mind over to Jesus
He wants to live in you,
Your prayers He will answer
He chose you to be one of the few.

You were born to seek and discover
let Christ absorb your every plea,
He made you for His purpose
so just ask and you will see.

Ask, ask, ask
let the Holy Spirit flow in thee,
Listen for the responsive love song
relax and let your heart believe!

A Strong Foundation

God is your Father
and Jesus Christ is His Son,
United and together
they declare that they are One.

They gave birth to the Holy Spirit
who abides within your heart,
Fulfilling God's abiding promise
to restore and set you apart.

When the Holy Spirit dwells within you
you gain power and strength from the start,
All setbacks you encounter
are overcome through your healing heart.

God knew what He was doing
when He heard your cry for aid,
For He made His home within you
His foundation had been laid!

Avoid Entrapment

When the heart and the mind are aligned
all other parts follow suit,
Connected and dependent on each other
they cooperate in harmonious pursuit.

Dysfunction arises when disconnected
seeking independence and going it alone,
Becoming trapped in self-destruction
and unable to remove the heavy stone.

Learning to love your neighbors
you must embrace them as your own,
To enhance your joy and well-being
join forces so you won't travel all alone!

Barbaric Terrorism

A barbarian is a crude uncouth person
lacking culture or refinement,
A member of an uncivilized people
seeking to destroy others as their primary assignment.

Islamists who believe a totalitarian culture
to be superior to free societies of Western civilization,
Seek destruction of opposing civilizations
making them, by definition, barbarians.

Christians who seek to live in obedience
to the commands of the Lord Jesus,
Seek not to conquer others
but to convert people to the faith that pleases.

For many years, we have believed that Islamic barbarians
were out there in far-distant places,
Barbarians are no longer far-distant
they are right here trying to displace us.

Islam, founded in the seventh century, was spread by the sword
with advancing hordes of warriors dispensing destruction,
In vast areas of the Middle East and North Africa
with minds focused on conquest with obsessive devotion.

The expansion of Islamic terrorism
is a long-established tide that threatens,
The barbarians are hell-bent on invasion
as they want to eliminate all religious competition.

As our civilization rushes toward collapse
what can we do to avert the destruction?
We need a new Reformation to awaken the West
and to repent from their own transgressions!

Be Still

The end is near
The beginning is long gone,
The time in between
Saw each day a new dawn.

As I approach the finish line
I see a light up ahead,
The few steps remaining
Across the line, I am led.

Soon I'll see victory
My destination will appear,
I'll walk through the gate
All will welcome me there.

I've been on a mission
And I've followed God's will,
My old life is ending
I can now rest and be still!

Be Strong

When you encounter trials and tribulations
and your faith won't sing its song,
Remember God has promised
and He says to you "be strong".

Your faith expands and prospers
when life tests your will to win,
Depend on the Holy Spirit
who grants new strength to begin again.

Your faith comes from the true source
which dwells within your heart,
Trust and believe in God's eternal promise
to overcome and never to depart.

God rescues with His strength from Heaven
listen to His words of peace,
Rest and overcome your weakness
and all your troubles will cease.

The Lord is your strength and your redeemer
He made and embraced you with His love song,
His power is made perfect in weakness
as your faith tests you to be forever strong!

Beauty's Imperfections

Inside all things in nature
there resides inclusions and imperfections,
Making them a thing of beauty
as God brings forth His perfect reflections.

The beauty that is seen by the beholders
could not reflect God's majesty,
Unless these unique and creative substances
contain the pure beauty of light's mystery.

Man himself is imperfect
and struggles to smile and embrace,
When God embeds His image in man's spirit
imperfections allow man to behold God's face.

Man loves and adores pure beauty
as God transforms our hearts with His grace,
He displays His beauty in nature
with His love for the human race!

Being Alive

As I march along life's highway
there's a bounce in every step,
There's a twinkle in my eye
as I feel alive and so adept.

As I greet those that pass by me
I smile and let them know,
That although we're only passing
it's good to see them on the go.

The beauty that surrounds me
I observe and give my thanks,
For as long as I'm rejoicing
I'm saving joy in my memory bank.

Being alive and feeling upbeat
allow me to lift my head up high,
As I march along life's highway
with my heart reaching to the sky!

Belonging

Your life belongs to God
it does not belong to you,
God's truth does not depend
on your own self-serving view.

Ask yourself what God would do
since He is the Savior of all mankind,
You were created in God's own image
you are not of your own design.

God cares where you spend eternity
just as your Father should,
Follow His light that leads you
believe that He provides all that's good

Be watchful and avoid false teachers
prosperity on earth must not be your goal,
God does not feed you through a cafeteria line
such temptations will not make you whole.

Your life on earth has a purpose
to be like Christ and to love your fellow man,
Absorb the true teachings of Jesus
all others put you in the sinking sand!

Bible Study

Why should I read the Holy Bible?
Because it contains God's story and advice,
Get started and focus on your assignment
As nothing else you could do will suffice.

Reading God's Word is a requirement
A continuous process with yourself in mind,
God's wants you to be His disciple
His plan and lessons are custom designed.

God conceived it, you must believe it
His message is loud and clear,
Follow where Jesus Christ leads you
And wash away all your fear!

Brand New

Nothing can separate us from the love of God
which is in Christ Jesus, our Lord,
Nothing in all created life
can overcome God's flaming sword.

The apostle Paul had experienced the truth
through a transformation process he had learned,
God's power and wisdom gave him understanding
and in his mind God's fire had burned.

Paul's conversion was transforming
his old mind had been made brand new,
He could see God's truth and purpose
and he knew what he had to do.

Nothing, I say nothing
can separate us from the love of God,
All praise, joy, and thanksgiving
I extend to Christ with my full applause!

Bright and New

Why, O Lord, don't we love on another?
Why do we choose our own way?
Why do we seek and do harm to others?
Don't we know that all were formed from the clay?

We put ourselves first and foremost
Seeing ourselves as superior to our neighbors,
Do we find great joy in the misery of others?
Bringing us no peace or restful slumber?

In our creative and righteous nature
We are to model our Lord and Savior,
He who aligned His heart and spirit
Being loving and of good behavior.

If you are confused, discouraged or off course
Repent and commence a brand-new stand,
Restore your mind and spirit
Begin again and take your Master's hand.

Discard your short-term vision
Bringing forth your long-term view,
It's your neighbors who will teach you
As you come forth bright and new!

Brothers Connected

What can I do to embrace my brothers?
the ones with opposing views?
Are they truly among my brothers?
and how can we both win and not lose?

The first step is to establish your foundation
those truths and laws you have found,
Then let your heart and mind absorb them
and then set them on Holy Ground.

When you travel on the risky roads of life
you are free to turn any way you choose,
When you know the destination you are seeking
you will remember what to accept and what to refuse.

You and your brothers are connected
you must face each other and debate the truth,
Your assignment on life's road to glory
requires all to embrace and join in the grand pursuit.

You and your brothers need each other
much more than you will ever know,
Your brothers can reinforce your mission
as the Holy Spirit directs the show!

Celebrate Life

You better get moving, time is in motion,
Have you chosen a new song, filled with all your devotion?

Are you ready to travel, and are your reservations complete?
Are you mentally ready, and can you truly compete?

Are you a born winner, or are you a loser, reborn?
Are you fearless in battle, even when tattered and torn?

Do you believe you are special, meant to climb the highest hill?
Do you possess the emotional makeup, without depending on a pill?

Do you know you're on assignment, with vision to see what's in store?
Do you sleep in peaceful slumber, knowing each new day is a gift to explore?

Do you understand teamwork, or do you seek to be on top?
Can you stand on your own two feet, or are you afraid you'll be a flop?

Were you an eager student, and do you have the skills to teach?
Can you explain what you are teaching, while not feeling, you must preach?

Are you willing to make a sacrifice, to ensure the greater good?
Can you still your mind and know, that Christ's truth lives under your hood?

Life is a celebration, made to praise and glorify,
Are you ready to be a leader, and lift others to soar and fly?

Chasing the Wind

I'm leaving and moving onward
and I'm inviting you to come along,
Don't bring any of your possessions
you'll be singing a brand-new song.

Your earthly treasures are meaningless
in the world where we are going to be,
You'll find more than you ever dreamed of
just come along and you will see.

The world you currently live in
is not where your heart will ascend,
Jump on the wagon to joy and happiness
and you will no longer be chasing the wind!

City of God

The city of Jerusalem
is known as God's city of peace,
The city established by David
where God's fullness would never cease.

God's promise first made to Abraham
would in time come into view,
First a temporary earthly city
to allow God's promise to become permanently true.

By faith the new city of Jerusalem
all gathered together will delight,
Until then may each be like Abraham
and live by faith, not sight!

Clouds

Clouds bring the mind of God
into spiritual reality,
There appears a rainbow after a rainstorm
as a sign of His covenant and dependability.

To understand and observe God's majesty
relax and drop all religious formalities,
So, you can clear the way for the Almighty
to fill your mind with His divine reality.

Clouds are formed between the earth and heaven
as if floating up in the air,
When looking upwards toward the heavens
on a cloud, Christ is sitting there.

Christ made His promises with authority
with His guarantee to all who are heavy laden,
He commanded the clouds above
and opened the doors of Heaven.

The world is now moving to a hosted service
allowing the truth to be available in the cloud,
As we advance in this new technology may we see
our future and our hearts forever proud!

Competition vs. Cooperation

Man has been taught to believe
he must learn to succeed with competition,
He sees himself as independent
without a need for cooperation.

To compete means survival of the fittest
so, you must do whatever it takes,
Winning is your defined mission
so, stand tall and protect all your stakes.

Competition does have its good points
by preventing size to dominate and rule,
Cooperation encourages unification and proving that
together you can become a useful tool.

Cooperation means believing in your brother
a turnaround from prior habits of your mind,
Winning doesn't mean separation, but giving
with unity room exists for all to shine!

Connected or Divided

Our God teaches and instructs us
that we are each connected to one another,
We are united in spirit and purpose
so we can love our neighbor like a brother.

By serving and completing acts of kindness
we contribute to the good of all,
By knowing our divine connection
we lift others so they won't fall.

As I observe the human condition
we have forgotten what God said we must do,
We now move in the opposite direction
not fruitful but spreading warfare and killing too.

Our world is truly divided
with a line drawn separating me from you,
We no longer love one another
intending to destroy the opposing point of view.

To live a full and joyous life
we must embrace our neighbors as ourselves,
Following God's laws and instructions
loving others like a bunch of happy elves!

Connected to My Father

God is my true Father
and I am His son,
We're marching together
our victory will be won.

United and fearless
the truth will be told,
Our eyes on the target
a new home we behold.

The Holy Spirit dwells in us
guiding our path,
Nothing can distract us
with joy we do laugh.

My life is a blessing
my Father's gift from above,
Our hands clasped together
with everlasting love.

God is my true Father
and I am His son,
We're marching together
our victory will be won!

Connecting Minds and Hearts

Progress involves a forward movement
which leaves the past behind,
Although the future is undefined
man must let the past unwind.

Man's progress of advancement
has left a trail of success and failure,
When looking back man discovers
his new direction is difficult to master.

During recent times man has advanced
with new technology and applications,
Creating an internet of people
communicating in new ways of satisfaction.

As man now enters the world of tomorrow
the things man has created and employed,
Are connecting with each other
as the internet of things is being deployed.

Man first learned to write and draw
next, came the printing press and he saw,
That he could communicate with each other
using a wireless process conceived in wonder and awe.

God first created the invisible network
which man is now beholding,
This network which man is deploying
connects with the cloud and cyberspace now unfolding.

Just as man's physical body is formed as a network
consisting of many parts,
By connecting to each other
they are directed by both minds and hearts!

Continuous Change

Conditions in my world
are in continuous change,
The priorities of yesterday
have now been rearranged.

To adjust to changing conditions
I let go of any fear,
I recall who I really am
God's child filled with hope and cheer.

The everlasting love of my Creator
brings peace of mind for me to see,
Protecting my eternal life
caressed with endless love for me.

The sun comes up and then goes down
ever adjusting to life's changing needs,
Breathing in and breathing out
as God discards the troubled weeds!

Creative Majesty

In the beginning
God's existence was without form,
His nature was as a spiritual being
and in truth He was perfectly adorned.

The truth that was His nature
needed to demonstrate itself,
By releasing and expressing
allowing His truth to display His wealth.

God is the seed of abundant love and purity
with desire to bear fruit to see,
The manifestation of His full nature
would reproduce all of His qualities.

Thought is the only mode of manifestation
expressing the Word of Divine Mind,
The purity and truth combine in perfect harmony
reproducing God's master design.

The purpose of God's spiritual being
was to give birth abundantly,
So, He could love, guide and protect
His creative majesty!

Discernment

There is a special skill
that each of us must learn,
It separates fact from fiction
this skill is called "discern".

The ability to make good judgements
requires knowledge of the truth,
With understanding and objectivity
you can employ your wisdom tooth.

Discernment is a practical ability
to distinguish right from wrong,
To discern means to detect with the senses
and not allow yourself to be strung along.

Don't be in a constant hurry
take your time to express concern,
Your choices really do matter
make sure you learn how to discern.

The ability to achieve discernment
requires your heart and mind to connect,
Let the Holy Spirit guide you
as all false thoughts, you eject!

Do You Believe?

The belief of many
is that all religions are the same,
The things they teach are similar
and lead to the same God who reigns.

The basic fact that separates us
and with confidence can be proclaimed,
Is that only Jesus Christ rose from the dead
the One who guarantees eternal life can be attained.

The evidence of Christ's resurrection
established Him as to only One who reigns,
Only He can deliver us from our sins
His resurrection allows new life to be sustained.

He is the hope to remove any obstacle
when He rose by removing the stone,
Jesus shed His blood so we could fully know Him
even as we are fully known.

The most important question you will ever answer
is "Do You Believe" that Jesus sacrificed His life is true?
And do you place your whole faith in His resurrection?
the One and only Lord who bled and gave His life for you!

Do You Know?

Do you know where you came from?
Do you know where you've been?
Do you know where you're going?
Will you lose or will you win?

Have you planned a trip or vacation?
Are your reservations intact?
Do you know how long you'll be gone?
Do you know when you'll be back?

Do you have an appointment?
Are you traveling alone?
Do you know where you'll be staying?
Will you be carrying your own cell phone?

Will someone meet and greet you?
Will you hug and kiss their face?
Will you both go out for dinner?
Will you bow your head when saying grace?

So many questions
So little time,
Don't forget to save some money
Even if it's only one small dime!

Don't Wait

When death is at your doorstep
and you don't know where to turn,
The time for your salvation
must be now so you won't burn.

Don't wait until it's too late
let your heart take full control,
Eternity is in your right hand
and holding your precious soul.

Christ is ready to lift you
into a new world beyond compare,
Put your faith and trust in His promises
and you will see how much He cares.

Life is not a guessing game
the truth is loud and clear,
Happiness is at your fingertips
live on and do not fear!

Don't Worry, Be Happy

Don't be anxious about anything
absolutely nothing should you fear,
Take your burdens to the Lord
then relax as you leave them there.

God is a specialist, so get specific
and ask God for what you want,
He will listen to your message
and will always be up front.

If God cares about the sparrow
surely, He must care about you too,
He is waiting to hear your voice
for He knows the choice is up to you.

A song written and sung by Bobby McFerrin
who sang "Don't Worry, Be Happy" my friend,
May these words continuously remind you
that God will knock on your door, so let Him in!

Eagle Eyes

When you observe your world from a distance
you can see all things from the air,
Like an eagle whose eyes are God's gift
that allow their wings to transcend despair.

When man stands close to the surface
things become bigger than they really are,
Best you lift yourself up to the clouds of heaven
then look down and view from afar.

Up close things can trap or block you
as they prevent a way to escape,
Adjust your perspective to be like the eagle
rise up and survey the landscape.

The eagle's keen sight and broad wings
permit a strong and soaring flight,
Let the eagle represent your power
to rise above and perceive God's holy light!

End Times

All beginnings have an ending
the Lord told us it was so,
God started and would finish
dropping the curtain and ending the show.

The wickedness of man
is great in the earth,
Man is surrounded with evil
end times will bring forth a new birth.

God calls believers to be watchful
and with our faith making a final stand,
More good times are coming
make ready for God's promised land.

God is alpha and omega
the beginning and the end,
He will fulfill each and every promise
on that you can depend!

Enjoy the Ride

Your journey through life
is a blessing you must employ,
As it teaches God's law of patience
so your heart and mind will fill with joy.

Enjoy the journey
don't miss the ride,
God is displaying His beauty
He is there by your side.

Life needs a destination
with a plan you can behold,
But don't be in a big hurry
just put your arrival on hold.

As you experience the journey
absorb all that you can,
As God prepares your destination
to accept and greet His loving fan.

God's plan needs to book your passage
and He's the driver who bled and died,
So discard your excess baggage
as you enjoy your journey's ride!

Experience the Moment

Experience the moment
don't let it slip by,
Absorb it intently
as you reach for the sky.

Devote your full attention
focusing on the task at hand,
Allow the result you are seeking
be the best that you possibly can.

Your mind is your servant
it follows your command,
Experience the moment
let the result meet your demand.

May the moments you've been granted
flow into your mind and hand,
So your heart can explode with gratitude
as God lifts you to the Promised Land!

Field of Battle

Life on earth is a battlefield
between the "haves" and the "have nots",
Both sides fight for position
to win victory and claim what they sought.

Once you choose the side you belong to
your position may never change,
For you are trapped and sealed in place
having entered your "home on the range".

Your loyalty is unforgiving
your vision is locked in place,
Division and lack of cooperation
insure neither side will ever embrace!

First Place

At the center of my attention
Jesus Christ is on my mind,
He is my focus when I wake up
He is the source of my love divine.

My life is like a sponge
that soaks up water within its folds,
To be filled with Christ's living water
lets me move forward as my world unfolds.

I have only one intention
only one which satisfies my thirst,
I shall live with Christ my Savior
and I will always put Him first!

Footsteps

Your feet establish a firm foundation
they hold you up and let you stand,
Your arch, heel, and toes are connected
allowing you to move about on God's precious land.

Your shoes are for protection
preventing hurts and also pain,
Yet when barefoot and unprotected
on Holy Ground, you encounter God's name.

Your feet are a source of motion
as they touch and move along,
Cherish them forever
as you march and sing your song.

The scriptures teach you to follow
and your feet enable you to move ahead,
Give thanks for your strong foothold
and follow where the Holy Spirit has led!

Forever Shine

There's a light that shines within you
a reflection of God's Son,
Where heaven's sun is forever shining
and you "in Christ" are truly one.

A place of peace and comfort
to rest and lay your head,
Where you can close your eyes
and see water flow through the valley's riverbed.

With closed eyes the sun continues
to shine brightly day and night,
While the moon is all its splendor
reflects God's sun until dawn's early morning light.

The sun's light dispels the darkness
as God's Son shines within your heart,
Forever throughout the ages
the Holy Spirit will never depart.

Both the sun and the Son are united
placing you at the head of the line,
Casting their rays of light
on you to forever shine!

From Faith to Following

Place your faith in Jesus alone
and turn from sin once and for all,
Now fully devoted as a follower of Christ
baptized by immersion as your name He did call.

Now get in the habit of a spiritual lift
a daily devotional and a quiet time that fits,
Feed on God's Word and write down your notes
speaking to your Savior is as good as it gets.

Christ is the Light that knows how to lead
embrace each encounter and surrender to God's will,
Moment by moment just follow His command
as you listen and allow your mind to be still.

Jesus is your Savior and he knows what to do
with love and devotion, He created the real you,
He leads the procession all day and all night
trust in Christ Jesus who will always follow through!

From the Ground Up

Your happiness comes
when your heart wants to fly,
Your joy comes when soaring
lifting you up to the sky.

The ground is your springboard
and is not your permanent domain,
Your stay here is temporary
your wings will lift you through the rain.

Your dream home awaits you
where all love does abide,
In peace, your heart keeps pumping
Christ's blood flowing on its joyride!

Full of Life

Each precious child of God is amazing
and truly full of life,
When a boy and girl are joined together
this can lead them to becoming man and wife.

If you are alive and reading these words
be careful and do not rock the boat,
Don't fight the upstream battle
if you want to remain afloat.

Life consists of risks galore
there are many ups and downs,
You must trust your inner signals
commit to go the full fifteen rounds.

Life requires much patience
and the courage to proceed,
To experience the fullness of living
you must let your inner child take the lead!

Full Price

Did you hear, that Christ is coming,
and He will be riding on a cloud?
The day is fast approaching
as I heard Him shout out loud.

He said to look up into the Heavens
rejoice knowing new life will soon begin,
For He comes to fulfill His promise
as He was sent to bring you back with Him.

All you have to do to ride His train to glory
is believe that Christ was sent for you,
No one cares for you more dearly
than the Lord whose love is true.

You have a new home that awaits you
so you can dwell forever in Paradise,
Get ready to be lifted up
by the One who bought your ticket
the Christ who paid full price!

Garden of Paradise

O Lord, I thank you
for my life here on precious earth,
The playground that you created
is so amazing since its birth.

The privilege to make my home here
is a blessing from a dream,
I'm so glad to dwell in your creation
set aglow from Heaven's light beam.

This paradise that I live in
from your mind, you did design,
So unique and picture perfect
no equal could I imagine or ever find.

I know my time on earth is limited
and soon my life here will end,
Yet the thrills and love you gave me
brought my cherished family and many friends.

Life's motion has no ending
and my soul and spirit will transcend,
I will greet you in the garden, Lord
your holy paradise without end!

Get Their Attention

Your purpose is to learn and to show
that you are unique and not like others you know,
You should not be controlled by uniformity
stand out and let your difference overcome conformity.

If you run an ad in a magazine
and want to ensure that it will be read,
Just print the ad upside down
letting your message come alive instead of dead.

To gain attention and be noticed in a crowd
you must not let conformity rule the day,
You are much more than just average
you are special and have important things to say.

Right action requires right timing
so best you be ready to shout,
Be prepared to rise to the occasion
and display your difference without any doubt.

The future belongs to those that seek
and to seek means to place yourself in full view,
Exposure is the key to gain attention
stay awake and let the world see the real you.

If you desire to reach a special destination
the road you travel must be your own,
The road on which all others are traveling
will not lead you to the place you call your home!

Give and Take

Our life includes
both give and take,
The taking is easy
with giving harder to participate.

Taking involves receiving
and a blessing to behold,
While giving is releasing
including your precious gold.

Taking can make you dependent
expecting more gifts to fill your store,
While giving lifts your spirit
allowing your heart to leap and soar.

Taking can turn to hoarding
possessing more than needs can bring,
Yet giving creates a yearning
causing your heart to rejoice and sing!

Give Yourself Away

When deciding your life's mission
plan on giving yourself away,
The more you give to others
the happier you will be each day.

Your treasure does not exist in possessions
your treasure abides in your heart,
The heart's capacity to store your treasures
holds more than all the world's shopping carts.

To reach your mission's destination
your arrival is in your own hands,
Each step on your journey's pathway is where
you will discover the treasures God has planned.

Material possessions are not lasting treasures
any value is unknown until released to stay,
If your barns are overflowing
it's time to give it all away.

You are not alone when on your mission
go forward and embrace each and every day,
Your true purpose is to share yourself with others
slow down and then give yourself away!

God Is...You Are

God is the subject
You are His expression,
God is the light
You are His reflection.

God is the sender
You are His receiver,
God calls the signals
You are His believer.

God is the author
You are His story,
God foretells the future
You are His glory.

God is the redeemer
You are His delight,
God is your Father
You are the child in His sight!

Godliness

Living a life of godliness
requires you to make a choice,
You can become a subject under God's control
or you can follow your own ringing voice.

Godliness is achieved through realization
and by continuous practice and repetition,
Godliness requires sacrifice
to bring about your own resurrection.

God is characterized by kindness
displayed by considerate and loving action,
His nature is to focus on good behavior
serving all Christians needing a strong attraction.

Developing and living a godly lifestyle
requires us to deny ourselves and follow Christ,
Focusing our thoughts on things above
and following Christ's empowering Light!

God's Laws

God's laws by definition
are established for all time,
His laws are unchanging
they are to be embedded in your mind.

His laws descend from His true character
they are not subject to change,
You can try to adjust or alter
but they will forever remain the same.

God's laws were established
and set forth in His "Word",
Both the Old and New Testament
convey His message to be heard.

The New Testament did not alter
it came forth to fulfill,
God's laws are unchanging
man's mind must climb the high hill.

All scripture is inspired by God's truth
given for correction and every good work,
Man is directed to learn and follow
God's laws he must not shirk.

Man is instructed to keep God's commandments
and to walk where Jesus walked,
Take the hand of God's Son and your Savior
and open your door when He arrives and knocks!

God's Word

Out of nothing God created something
all that He made was first imaged in His mind,
Like the lilies of the field
each uniquely made and one of a kind.

Humankind is God's ultimate creation
dependent on God to sustain all of life,
From food for the body to music for the soul
God loved life so dearly, He made both man and wife.

God knew man needed a playground
to enjoy the fruits of God's green earth,
So He created earth and also heaven
knowing man needed both to grow from birth.

God recorded His amazing story
in the Holy Bible know as His "Word",
So man could grow in true wisdom
choosing everlasting life through the story he heard!

Habits

Habits are those things ingrained in you
the things that define who you are,
They were programed in your inner mind
when you practiced becoming a star.

Habits can be good or bad
either to help you or drag you down,
Good habits can be your servant
where bad habits allow you to drown.

A habit takes only a few weeks to be planted
becoming firmly rooted in an automatic zone,
Use caution when growing your garden
plant only good seeds to be sown.

The choice is yours for the asking
so be careful what you choose,
The key to the good habits you're seeking
determines if you win or if you lose!

Hacking

The term "hacking" means to invade
a place where you should not be,
To infiltrate and spy
on another person's privacy.

The hacker's best intensions
are to embarrass and to expose,
By taking confidential information
first twist and then disclose.

This information disclosed is disruptive
and causes no means of good cheer,
To enter another's domain without invitation
exposes what a hacker must not hear.

In the wireless world of cyberspace
it may be difficult to protect your secrecy,
As long as the hacker's plan of action
makes it hard to track their identity.

It is best to safeguard your secrets
and it's best to keep hackers away,
Give thought where you store your treasures
so you can keep all hackers at bay!

Heavy Traffic

As I drive along the roadway
with heavy traffic all around,
Wondering when I will make it
to the place where I'm bound.

Many cars do surround me
I see red lights flashing up ahead,
I wonder if an accident
has left somebody dead.

I soon hear a loud siren
wailing through the air,
I question my own judgement
or why I'm stuck here.

I'm stressed out with frustration
I start pulling out my hair,
I'll be late for my appointment
is there someone else who truly cares?

Trying to remain calm during chaos
I try to relax and be still,
Asking God to come to my rescue
since I can't climb this high hill.

Soon the traffic starts moving
and I'm picking up speed,
I'm thinking that I might make it
I'm thanking God for addressing my need!

Hidden Treasure

The answers lie hidden
awaiting to be found,
Like a treasure that is buried
below the surface of the ground.

Whatever you are seeking
it wants you to find,
You must seek where it is hiding
you must explore your inner mind.

The treasure you are seeking
lies just beyond the cloudy haze,
Close your eyes and see the treasure
let it reward you and amaze.

The most rewarding treasure
is not so far away,
Hidden from the outside
as your inner vision shows the way!

His House

Christ makes His home within you
and He calls it "His House",
It is where He moves and has His being
where His peace cannot disturb even a mouse.

Christ loves all of His brethren
and His desire is to be close and true,
He chose to be always present
so He made His house and home within you.

Your Lord loves you dearly
His promises go beyond His very best,
He has guaranteed to lift your spirits
He will fulfill all of His Father's requests.

The dwelling place of your Lord and Savior
the place where He makes His home base,
It's where you can meet and with arms wide open
where you both can reach out and embrace.

In the outside world we live in
the church is established as "His House",
Where man can greet his neighbor
as the Lord unites us eliminating all doubt!

Home Is Where the Heart Is

My heart is most secure
where it makes its home,
Where it can rest in peace
and know it's not alone.

The rhythm of my heartbeat
can continue without travail,
When in the blessed comfort
of its home where it will prevail.

My heart is also the place
where Jesus Christ makes His home,
So, He and I can rest together
and never be alone.

My heart is relaxed and upbeat
when home resting in its bed,
Where it is forever reminded
to comfort my precious Jesus' head!

Hope

Hope is the seed of progress
it builds and expands to become more,
When planted in fertile soil
it brings forth what your mind had in store.

Hope is your personal promise
that your dreams can reach wide and far,
Where Heaven releases its blessings
and hope sends you beyond where you are.

Hope is a primary ingredient
a key part of your recipe for success,
You can magnify and reach your destination
when hope rises to bring you the best.

Hope is the vision of your future
that inspires you to rise and to seek,
Hope is the inspiration you are seeking
so relax and take a fresh peek!

How Time Flies

How time flies
it moves so fast,
Its wings are strong
each second can't last.

When you blink your eyes
your life sings along,
The song you are singing
will not be remembered for long.

Time cannot be saved
nor can it be stored,
Nothing can contain it
or hold back with a magic cord.

Time is an illusion
it wasn't really there, you know?
First it happens and then it's gone
continuously abiding only in its flow!

Important Questions

Do you know your Father who made you?
Do you know just who you are?
Do you know you were made in His image?
Do you know you are one who wears the star?

Did you know that early this morning,
when you awakened and jumped out of bed?
That the One who awakened and watches over you
is the One who gave His life for you and bled?

Your challenges are assigned in pieces
with each one teaching about who you are,
As you complete each assignment you were given
you can rise up on one of God's shooting stars.

Do you have what it takes?
Can you in good faith follow the King, and serve?
Are you willing to give yourself to Christ?
Are you ready to sacrifice and test your nerve?

God's promises are true and perfect
His plan was conceived with you in mind,
His desire is for you to trust Him and believe
that His love is the best you'll ever find!

Inside Job

You are a spiritual being
you are the object of God's love and power,
God formed you from inside His heart
in the beginning at the earliest hour.

Creation begins by planting a seed
first in mind and then in fertile ground,
Where God can nurture and bless
igniting a spark and letting its flame abound.

All growth proceeds and advances
from the center or heart inside at rest,
Then when awakened it springs forth
expressing the true love that will bless.

God knew that He must place Himself
where His love would expand and grow,
So, He chose to make His blessed home in you
where His amazing love would eternally flow!

Isolation

Many people will try it
believing they can make it alone,
They refuse to depend on others
living on both ends of the phone.

Their perspective has become distorted
they withdraw and turn to pills,
They fall into addiction
searching for others to cure their ills.

Trapped in a world of selfhood
they lose sight of their identity,
Soon they can't twist the doorknob
being caught up in twilight's reality.

Be careful what you wish for
soon it may appear at your door,
You must learn to depend on others
so you can rise up off the floor!

I Thank Him

When I think about the Lord
I feel His strong magnetic force,
Guiding my direction
and keeping me on the right course.

The Lord surrounds my entire being
and He dwells within my heart,
His blood erased all my shortcomings
His grace promised His love would not depart.

How can I thank Him
for loving me so perfectly?
I will adore Him forever
and praise Him throughout eternity!

It's Your Choice

Jump on the bandwagon
join the right team,
Do you want to be a winner?
are you pursuing your amazing dream?

The process of awakening
requires a choice that depends on you,
If you want to move forward
you must think like winners do.

Out with the garbage
and up goes the cream,
Your mind seeks new direction
when you follow God's bright sunbeams.

There is a brighter day coming
momentum is building a force,
You must join with the winners
to lift you spirit without remorse.

The choice you'll be making
can bring joy with the rain,
By joining a team of winners
brings a world that you can claim!

Join in the Battle

Did you know that a battle is going on?
and you are being recruited to join in?
The truth team's logo is the cross
the one on which Christ Jesus died so you could win.

The battle is between the light and the darkness
the power of truth against the deceit of evil's lie,
Your plane to victory is ready for takeoff
it's on the runway, full of fuel, and ready to fly.

The army of darkness includes many soldiers
who have been fed a most destructive lie,
Taught to believe in an illusion
to conform or most assuredly they must die.

Your beliefs control your actions
So, make sure you embrace Christ's light,
Reject all false illusions from the dark side
and glorify the truth as you prepare to fight!

Keep On

Stay strong...Stay fit
Keep on moving...Present your case,
Redeemed through faith
Saved by grace.

Storms will confront you
Do not fear...Christ will erase,
Redeemed through faith
Saved by grace.

Move on forward
Keep up the pace,
Redeemed through faith
Saved by grace.

Hold Christ's hand
Let His arms embrace,
Redeemed through faith
Saved by grace.

Paradise awaits you
Let peace form a base,
Redeemed through faith
Saved by grace!

King of Glory

Do you have a King in your life,
one who reigns supreme?
A King unlike any other,
a King who is able to redeem?

There is such a King at your doorstep
one who can capture your heart and mind,
One who is righteous and victorious
ruling with love for all time.

This King exists at the center of your being
where His love invites you into His kingdom,
So, you can experience the joys of expression
and celebrate His almighty dominion.

The one King that's in charge of His kingdom
the only One who deserves to wear the crown,
Behold the majesty of Jesus, the Christ
the only One who will never let you down.

Jesus rode into Jerusalem on a donkey
not to conquer the city like an earthly king,
But to conquer your heart and mind
and lead you to the glory only He could bring!

Lessons

Lessons represent instructions
designed to inform and teach,
As a student present in the classroom
the instructor does not need to preach.

Lessons appropriate for the students
form building blocks with more to come,
Step by step they build a tower
standing tall and that can never be undone.

Lessons learned must excite the senses
causing a thirst to dive in deep,
By focusing on the lessons before you
you can retain, honor, and forever keep.

Life consists of many choices
and seeking knowledge can make you wise,
Dive in and employ all your senses
and master the lessons so you can win the prize!

Let Your Heart Sing

Your heart is the center of all of life
and the blood of Christ's spirit is alive,
With its continuous rhythm and beat
God's song guarantees you will survive.

Your heart is where your strength lies
it's the secret place of the Most High,
The Lord is your refuge and your fortress
He will hear you every time you cry.

Do not be afraid of the terror of darkness
listen to the song your heart sings,
The Lord shall cover you with his feathers
and protect you under His wings!

Life's Equation

Honoring life's equation
is the way that leads to peace,
Balancing in concert
man's fears and wars will surely cease.

With giving on the left side
and receiving on the right,
Both support the other
essential to bring delight.

Like seeds that grow and prosper
each multiplying what it is,
Connecting to each other
With what is yours is also his.

Giving means releasing
opening the doorway to receive,
Completing life's equation
for those who in Christ believe!

Life's Fragments

Life is made up of many fragments
with some lasting a brief period of time,
A fragment can be easily remembered
when an emotion is fixed in your mind.

Life's experiences come about through observation
and when you participate, placing yourself on the line,
The best learning experience you can entertain
are those that produce an everlasting sign.

Your life insists on progress
which you won't experience by standing still,
One day in each week is reserved for resting
and each night your dreams can produce a thrill.

Your purpose in life is progressive
you are alive in a world of change,
Your clock's hands are moving around the circle
you must adjust and quickly change lanes.

Since life means you are in motion
and motion means to continuously change,
Best you take notes and try to remember
those times when storm clouds brought the rains!

Living Waters

There are two sides of the river
with dry land on either side,
Both sides depend on the flowing water
to sustain life, to maintain, and to abide.

Central to all the living
is the water passing through,
With its motion ever-flowing
making life a joyous rendezvous.

Man cannot live without water
it's the source that makes life whole,
As both sides of the river's waters
drink its magical refreshing flow.

As the river passes through
man's sacred and blessed domain,
The river needs both sides
so God can fulfill His promise to sustain.

Jesus said "If anyone is thirsty
let him come to me and drink",
Believers are offered living water
to discover the missing link!

Love in Action

My life is a loving splendor
cascading all over me,
First, God sent my parents
who blessed and gave me the key.

Throughout my years of upward growth
including some pain and fears,
My many friends and neighbors
brought an endless stream of cheers.

I have some glorious children
the number of them is three,
They stood by with love and honor
sending pure love gifts for me to see.

Then along came my grandkids
six of them in all,
They bring me so much joy
watching them learn and grow up tall.

The more I extend my love and blessings
to those I truly love and adore,
The love I receive back in return
becomes more, more, and more.

There are countless souls that love me
and I bless each and every one,
But none of them could ever love me
without the love of God's only Son!

Love's Light

God has truly blessed me
when on me He cast His light,
He placed me in my earthly home
and told me, all was right.

He taught me how to follow
the colors of the bright rainbow,
Where I would discover my treasure
where His light had cast a shadow.

The peace of God, my Father
lifts me where I want to be,
Forever in His presence
magnified for all to see.

God has led me to His living water
to satisfy my thirst,
Where He infuses me with His magic
His essence at my birth.

I know God's light is present
for I see it everywhere,
He loves me as He blesses
and I know how much He cares!

Love's Splendor

O Lord, you have made and placed me
at the foot of all your glory,
Where my eyes can behold, and understand
hearing your Word which tells your true story.

I know I can trust and depend on
your Word I have studied and heard,
I can feel your amazing love
as pure as a song from a chirping bird.

I believe in your dominion
I believe in your strength and power,
I delight as I walk in your blessed garden
I need your arms around me, each and every hour.

I'm amazed at your creation
seeing your overwhelming masterpiece,
But most of all I thank you
for granting to me, your peace and eternal grace!

March with You to Glory

Jesus, Jesus
mighty is your name,
You have touched me with your essence
and without you I would go insane.

Your righteousness surrounds me
I feel your warm embrace,
Your strength and your compassion
demonstrate your blessed grace.

I do not ask for mercy
as I slow down to your steady pace,
For my mind is clearly focused
as I seek to kiss your loving face.

Everything I have longed for
my mind and heart forms the perfect view,
I commit my life and mission
as I praise and worship you.

I will join your mighty army
and I will defend your precious name,
I will march with you to glory
and I will never be the same!

Mental Adjustment

If you believe in a liberal agenda
you must wake up and realize,
That your wonder days are over
you will never claim them back.

Your comrades are deserting
as they have had it with their show,
They are leaving their seats in the theater
they want to go where the true wind blows.

You must not try chaos and destruction
you should not rebel and attack,
You must get in line and follow
so, we can deliver what you lack.

Your future requires a present adjustment
your thinking must not experience more decline,
We present a new opportunity
to transform your misguided state of mind!

Mind Action

The law of God is order
working out the principle of being,
Bringing divine ideals into manifestation
through the steps of creativity.

All limitations in the world are the result
of man's error thoughts and beliefs,
Only spiritual things are eternal
as God's creative process will never cease.

The law of mind action
consists of mind, idea, and then manifestation,
First is the mind, and then the idea
and finally, manifestation completes its expression.

Serving the Lord requires the keeping of divine law
through meditating on spiritual ideals,
God's laws are written on the heart of man
by the Truth which only God reveals!

Motion

The wind doth blow
and the flowers grow,
The rising sun begins the show
and the moon reflects its cool white glow.

The earth spins
and gravity holds us in,
The clock's hands go around
as man walks on holy ground.

The cycle of life
is in a rhythm of its own,
Created by the Master
so man never walks alone!

Moving On

At first I ride in a baby carriage
then I advance to a tricycle,
As soon as I outgrow it
I move on to a bicycle.

The next ride that will carry me
is a four-wheel automobile,
Then on to a truck that's much bigger
to a walker then then a wheel chair.

As you grow your vehicle grows with you
since your larger size dictates a change,
Accept the change and embrace it
let go of the past, adapt and rearrange.

Life is like a moving target
to lift you off your toes,
Don't fight the wheels that carry you
because life knows where it goes!

Music and Laughter

The two main ingredients in the bounty of life
are laughter and music's amazing sounds,
The seven musical notes and five sharps and flats
a total of twelve, fulfilling Spirit's glorious crown.

Laughter provides relief from pressure
causing the mind to relax and slow,
Giving the heart an injection
lifting the mind to produce a refreshing glow.

Musical notes are based
on relative harmonic frequencies,
Creating an infinite number of possible notes
all representing spiritual realities.

The seven natural notes
display the divine law of perfection,
and twelve represents spiritual fulfillment,
By combining laughter and music
you can experience life's key to enjoyment!

My Loving Mother

My mother was a saintly soul
she was truly other-centered,
She blessed me as she loved me
knowing I needed to be mentored.

She brought forth my brother, my sister, and I
she was family all the way,
She was always where I could find her
she nurtured and protected as we prayed.

Her hands were always busy
for she accomplished numerous tasks,
Her capabilities were endless
and she never wore any confusing masks.

My mother came down from Heaven
and she knew what she must do,
She believed in her assignment
as she loved me through and through!

New Birth

There's a popular belief
that a change will come,
To believers, born of Spirit,
reborn after they are dead and gone.

There is a "New Birth" that comes
right here and now,
Living inside man's spirit
where he repents, and makes his vow.

Man must be lifted up
a spiritual process being "born anew",
As a new life of harmony
casts off the old and presents the new you.

New birth can be explained
when man's spirit, soul, and body are transformed,
Reborn and made a new creature
while Gabriel blows his horn!

New Dawn

From His arms ... to His arms
throughout all of eternal time,
You must understand God's message
God is perfect, holy, and divine.

God has made no mistakes
in the past, present, or future,
God created the heavens and the earth
then He made you to love and to nurture.

To fuel your growth and progress
you must flood your mind with hope,
Read and study God's Holy Word
which describes what you need to cope.

Meekness is not the same as weakness
power does not mean to devour,
Your strength lies in your humanity
when you display your blooming flower.

The past is the road you've traveled
your future is the road you'll be on,
The direction you'll be going
will determine if you'll reach the new dawn!

No Two Alike

Everything that God created
everything He called by name,
In a world of similarity
nothing is exactly the same.

Duplication through reproduction
God's plan was set in motion,
Every kind and every species
follows suit without confusion.

From the human voice to a fingerprint
a snowflake or the petal of a flower,
Each unique from any other
standing tall in its own special tower.

In the past, present, and future
God made each thing unique,
No two will ever be alike
the twain shall never meet.

Inside the core of being
God place the seed from up above,
So, the fruit of every living thing
could reflect God's never-ending love!

Obstructions of the Mind

The lessons of life
are learned through absorption,
Your mind is like a sponge
soaking up love's full devotion.

Nature deplores a vacuum
and must draw in to fill up the hole,
To allow new thought to enter
first discard what obstructs the flow.

Your faith will produce your victory
as your belief first sets the stage,
Practice releasing all thoughts that hold you
so new thoughts can replace and truly amaze.

The truth of God will never forsake you
your right choice is what it will take,
Like a sponge that is seeking living water
let your mind and heart be lifted up and awake!

Old Time Gospel Hymns

"I LOVE TO TELL THE STORY"
back when I was a "WAYFARING STRANGER",
"ON JORDAN'S STORMY BANKS"
where "I SURRENDERED ALL" from danger.

I had "JUST A LITTLE TALK WITH JESUS"
and discovered "THERE IS POWER IN THE BLOOD",
I felt His "BLESSED ASSURANCE" saying
"SHALL WE GATHER AT THE RIVER" after the flood?

"HE LEADETH ME" on "HOLY GROUND"
"BECAUSE HE LIVES", "IT IS WELL WITH MY SOUL",
"A MIGHTY FORTRESS IS OUR GOD"
"IN THE SWEET BY AND BY" He made me whole.

"ALL HAIL THE POWER OF JESUS' NAME"
"TIS SO SWEET TO TRUST IN JESUS",
"LEANING ON THE EVERLASTING ARMS"
"JUST AS I AM" God sees us.

Thank you Lord Jesus
for leading me "WHERE THE SOUL NEVER DIES",
"I AM BOUND FOR THE PROMISED LAND"
your "AMAZING GRACE" gave me wings to fly!

One Step Ahead

Making progress
requires staying ahead,
The forces behind you
want to put you to bed.

Staying out front
requires a preset mind,
The finish line in focus
leaving all others far behind.

Winners learn quickly
to stay one step ahead,
After crossing the finish line
they collapse into a feather bed!

On Life's Battlefield

Each of us are agents of change
responsible for changing hearts and minds,
Loving others as we love ourselves
signaling with our thumbs-up and high signs.

We are cornerstones for progress
for church, family, friends, and neighbors,
Serving our Lord and Savior
presenting His pure love and favors.

Take the Lord's hand and let Him lead you
going into battle means loving the cause,
You are a soldier in God's army
let His Holy Word speak without a pause.

Listen to the commands that come forward
without fear your faith will expand,
Your strength will rise to the occasion
and your victory will forever stand!

Onward and Upward

What is meant by "Everlasting"?
and what does "Forever" say?
What happened to the final curtain?
is life more than a three-act play?

What is meant by "It's Over"?
does life abruptly end?
Is there more to come tomorrow?
is there a surprise around the bend?

When life is abundantly happy
and you don't want it to end,
Why does our body quit working?
when our spirit knows how to transcend?

God created the human body
so man could learn from the outside in,
Once he learned about the senses
he would seek the truth that is hidden within.

Life consists of stages
growing one step at a time,
Once you complete all the courses
you can give up your body for the divine

In God's kingdom, His reign is everlasting
and is not comparable to the world you now know,
His kingdom has no ending
new stage, same director, and all go!

Our Enemy

Life presents man with many problems
that he blames on an outer source,
Each trouble that confronts him
must delay and take its course.

Man believes in self-protection
and will use what comes in view,
He wants to believe what's honest
yet he will twist what he knows is true.

Without the truth presented
man suffers and must pay what's due,
When he forms a coalition to support him
he begins to believe his lies are true.

Enemies can come from the outside
but the challenges come forth from inside,
Division becomes an obsession
so the battle rages on and intensifies.

The solution to life's problems
is to apply what Christ advised,
Let your heart, soul, and mind love the Lord, thy God
and love your neighbor as thyself on both sides!

Perfection

Perfection is an objective achievement
a goal and an effort to eliminate error,
As you attempt to achieve your objective
mentally walking the straight and narrow.

Perfection is a misunderstood achievement
since only God can make things come true,
Perfection includes many errors
which allows the target to come into view.

To achieve any objective
Imperfections are embedded in your goal,
When complete with frame and signature
They lift up your heart and soul!

Perspective

To avoid most obstructions
you must see like very few,
You must not get lost in the forest
where the trees can block your view.

You can see beyond the horizon
which is closer than you think,
When you perceive that you are far away
you won't discover the missing link.

Your vision can predict your future
which can be both near and far,
Even the far-distant nighttime splendor
won't prevent you from touching a star.

Moses led his people
across the deep Red Sea,
Where his vision of the other side
told him they were meant to be!

Positive Guidelines

Seeing...Believing; Seeking...Finding

Hoping...Praying; Loving...Everlasting

Giving...Receiving; Sharing...Caring

Living...Being; Admiring...Adoring

Doing...Fulfilling; Conceiving...Manifesting

Hearing...Trusting; Dreaming...Empowering

Belonging...Restoring; Satisfying...Glorifying

All the above are acts of expressing
revealing your best innermost thought,
Helping you to look upward
and claim your eternal spot!

Precious Gifts

Two of God's precious gifts
are laughter and music's sweet flow,
Laughter to lift your spirits
and music to fire up your soul.

To be without either one
your life would be incomplete,
So let your funny bone be plugged in
so your heart can relax in your recliner seat.

Music is God's sweet medicine
and laughter relieves stress and sets you free,
God promised exactly what is needed
to enjoy life to the fullest degree!

Precious Hearts

I spent some time with my granddaughters
so I could plant some special seeds,
I wanted them to learn the truth
and how they could perform great deeds.

You must first love your heavenly Father
with all your strength and might,
Then love your neighbors as yourself
each morning, all day long, and during the night.

God's Holy Spirit dwells within you
to guide, comfort, and learn,
Your assignment is to use your talents
to help others with each good turn.

You are a child of your heavenly Father
and He has blessed you with His best,
Give thanks for all His blessings
then let your heart do all the rest.

The seeds that I am planting
will give my granddaughters a head start,
Building within good seeds of truth
to empower their precious hearts.

Oh, precious hearts
how very much I do love thee,
For you are the beauty of each morning
sending your light and love right back to me!

Press On

Life on earth brings interruptions
circumstances that distract your vision,
"Press on" toward your goal and make it personal
with your focus to win victory in Heaven.

Victory comes to those who are ready
to those who follow and pursue,
By straining to reach your destination
forget the past and replace it with the new.

Singleness of mind prevents distractions
your obsession must rule both day and night,
No delays or sidetracks can prevent you
as you *"press on"* with the finish line in sight.

To *"press on"* means to move forward
to decisively commit and to take hold,
You can win the greatest prize imagined
knowing Christ Jesus, the Master to behold!

Pure Love

As I watched my young granddaughters
grow in the world of make-believe,
They were fascinated with Christmas time
as the trusted and perceived.

They wrote their letters to Santa
as they sought gifts from the North Pole,
Their purity and faith in Christmas
lifted up my heart and soul.

Young minds need to behold the magic
and the mystery of all-consuming love,
So as they grow in wisdom and stature
becoming like their Heavenly Father above.

Watching my granddaughters mature
is a memory I'll cherish and keep aglow,
They have brought me so much joy and pleasure
as I watched their magic show.

The birth of Jesus Christ
will be cherished till the end of time,
As He lifts the hearts of children
as tells them they are mine!

Promised Land

The Promised Land
is where you belong,
It's not where you're going
love placed you there with a nursery song.

It's not over the mountain
or the valley below,
It's wherever you are
you are eternal and forever whole.

Seeking is not about searching
it's God's assignment to make you strong,
You must establish a foundation
so you can learn about right and wrong.

In the Promised Land, you'll find perfection
by claiming your God-given gift,
In the Garden of Eden
it's where God will uplift!

Refining Your Thoughts

The mind is a reservoir
its capacity is great,
It stores what it's given
all comes through its gate.

The key to mental storage
is to first filter the flow,
Let the heart purify
sending forth the best of show.

Don't let the wrong thoughts
enter the mind,
Allow only the good thoughts
with pure love so refined.

Be careful which tree
from the garden you eat,
Follow God's instructions
so, you can surely repeat.

Let love be your mission
with your heart just be kind,
Loving your Lord and your neighbor
with what's stored in your mind!

Reflecting the Light

God's purpose in creating light
was to wake up the world from darkness,
Darkness has no inherent energy
and cannot stand in the light of day.

Light comprises wisdom and understanding
and illuminates the mind of mankind,
Light is faith and belief in action
revealing the path man can seek and can find.

Darkness hides in the shadows
and is unable to exist in the light of day,
God's sun is continuously shining
and His Only Son reflects God's loving way.

Your eyes are your tool for vision
and vision shows the truth of who you are,
Light eliminates fear and confusion
so man can reflect God's brightest star!

Release Your Power

Accept yourself for who you are
all decisions are up to you,
The changes you decide are yours to make
no opinions of others will do.

Success requires your faith in self
with a foundation of courage and respect,
Your inner spirit must be set ablaze
as you continue on down the track.

At times life may seem confusing and unfair
yet hard times are meant for you to grow,
Boldly live with your inner passion
release your power and let it flow.

Your ship rests at anchor
awaiting your supreme command,
Lift up your spirit and start sailing
so your future will be simply grand!

Remove This Stone

If you feel you are living behind a stone
where guilt, doubt, and despair block you in,
You need not be overwhelmed or give up
for there is One who can overcome and let you win.

Deliverance is achieved through resurrection
a power source with amazing strength,
By rolling away the stone that blocked His tomb
the Lord was lifted up so He would not sink.

Jesus overcame the massive stone
that prevented Him from returning from the dead,
God blessed Him when He persevered through trial
and He sacrificed the blood which He shed.

Blessed are the ones who persevere under trial
having stood the test for a time,
They will receive the crown of glory
from the Lord who promised they would shine!

Repetition

Repetition is an essential part of communication
to get through the complications of the mind,
To gain the understanding of your target audience
requires duplication to penetrate and align.

Typically, the mind does not remember
and when it does it quickly forgets,
Repetition reinforces previous messages
as they are recorded where the sun never sets.

Repetition is God's plan to change behavior
as His story is repeated over and over again,
The Gospel repeats His message throughout the ages
to be established in the recesses of the human mind!

Restoration

"Water" represents many aspects
including thoughts that conform to environment,
Every thought leaves its form in consciousness
as water gathers in holes of confinement.

When a flood of negative thought sweeps over us
we become discouraged and want to give up,
Being scared that trouble lies up ahead
without the Truth, the water's flow can't interrupt.

When water's flow returns to natural channels
our strength and faith are restored,
We return as the living water escapes confinement
and our lives can again be adored!

Saying Goodbye

I want to live
I'm not ready to die,
My unfinished business
Requires adjusting my bow tie.

I must be ready
I must look my best,
The place I am going
Invites me to be their guest.

Many will greet me
The stadium will be packed,
I must prepare and get ready
As they welcome me back.

The stars that shine brightly
And light up the sky,
Are calling me homeward
As my past says goodbye!

Say "Yes"

Say "Yes" to the present moment
it is all you'll ever have,
Make it your primary focus
accept "now" as your healing salve.

Your mind may be full of static
causing pain to interfere,
Slow down and calm your emotions
be quiet and let God's music come in clear.

The roar that you hear inside you
cannot represent truth God sees in your heart,
Unplug the energy that feeds your mind
and enjoy a brand-new start.

The past and the future
don't represent who you truly are,
Tap into your inner dimension
say "yes" to "now" and you'll go far!

Search or Claim

From appeasement to empowerment
stand up for what you believe,
Others will respect your purpose
when the truth is what you conceive.

To stand up you must first show up
and be firm so all can see,
If you decide to draw a red line
make sure you will honor your decree.

Quit searching for what you don't have
and claim what you hold in your hand,
Let the world know you mean business
as you stand tall in God's marching band!

See and Know

The things of this world
have both a front and a back,
Until you see both sides
there is something that you lack.

When viewing only from the outside
you still are missing the complete view,
Yet when you can see from the inside
you can behold a better you.

Your mind is fueled by wisdom
waiting for you to know,
The truth of your full potential
is to learn and continue to grow.

As you sit in the driver's seat
with the steering wheel in both hands,
Keep your eye on the road ahead
to ensure you'll know where to land!

Seven Steps

Listening leads to learning

Learning leads to wisdom

Wisdom leads to belief

Belief leads to faith

Faith leads to transformation

Transformation leads to salvation

Salvation leads to resurrection

These seven steps around the circle
Expressing God's amazing grace!

Side by Side

The battlefield awaits you
you must enter the fray,
The noise must be stopped
to bring forth a new day.

Your courage is needed
the enemy is advancing in hordes,
You must rise up and get moving
before they strike with their swords.

The new day awaits you
and all others on your team,
The sun will bring its mighty power
through its bright penetrating sunbeams.

You are a vital part of the answer
to assure victory is won,
Join the team wearing all the ribbons
ride side by side with God's almighty Son!

Solutions

What are you worried about?
and why do you fret and stew?
Do you know you can solve all your problems?
by letting your perception take an uplifting view?

In the outside world you live in
all things exist for only a time,
Soon your current dilemma
will pass through leaving no hill to climb.

Worry results from anxiety
fearing the worst will surely come,
The troubles you believe are at your doorstep
are most likely to dissolve and come undone.

Learn to love and accept your situation
loving means not paying attention to time,
New direction is the Lord's gift of perspective
where your mind, heart and thoughts will align.

If your worrisome thoughts are depressing
and your frown is now out of style,
Go look at yourself in a mirror
and let your face commence to smile!

Song of Praise

I can hear God singing
He is releasing from His heart,
He made me out of nothing
He gave me a glorious start.

He showered me with His blessings
everything I could ever need,
He took the essence of His own heart
and He placed it in my seed.

He taught me to appreciate
the world in which I was placed,
He guided me to the King who sacrificed
giving His life to bless me with His grace.

I am filled and overflowing
with my eternal song of praise,
God and I have joined together
as He continues to amaze!

Songs of Sunshine

"Good Morning Starshine"
"It's a Beautiful Morning",
"Here Comes the Sun"
"A New Day is Dawning".

"Sunshine on My Shoulders"
"Under the Sun",
"Let the Sunshine In"
where I am "One with the Sun".

"Morning Has Broken"
"Keep on the Sunny Side",
"I Can See Clearly Now"
"I'll Follow the Sun" and abide.

"You Are My Sunshine"
I need the "Sunshine of Your Love",
"Brighter than Sunshine"
"Let the Sunshine In" from Heaven above.

With a "Pocketful of Sunshine"
from "That Lucky Old Sun",
"The Warmth of the Sun"
proves my victory is won!

Sound Choices

You are your own best advisor
the one that makes the choice,
Others may introduce their opinions
yet the decision comes through your voice.

You are in charge of your present
which affects your future goals,
Today's decisions belong to your future
best your path not be filled with holes.

Your choices are of high importance
only you can rule both day and night,
Choose a spiritual source to guide you
and His name is Jesus Christ!

Speaking the Truth

If your mind is somewhat off center
and is not forming constructive pictures,
I would suggest you take a break
pick up your Bible and read some scripture.

Your mind is your greatest blessing
it absorbs what you serve on its plate,
It brings forth whatever you feed it
it confirms exactly what it ate.

The human mind follows instructions
our good Lord designed it that way,
Even if garbage is what you put in it
the same comes out no matter what you say.

Best you fill your mind with scripture
if you want to shout out the truth,
By filling your mind with rich blessings
you'll sleep well and reproduce ripe fruit!

Start and Stop

Start doing what is right
and stop doing what is wrong,
Right is right and wrong is wrong
this is the truth so make it your song.

When things are out of balance
and harmony cannot be found,
Give thanks for your understanding
then produce a brand-new sound.

The secret to all new beginnings
is to release the past and let it go,
Then the vacuum you've created
allows the new to become the show.

The song you have been singing
must be out of tune,
So, take a needed rest stop
and let your high note reach the moon!

Strength

Size is not a sign of strength
nor does size confirm you are physically fit,
Victory through strength belongs
to the person who will not quit.

Determination alone is omnipotent
it depends on your heart and brain,
Your attitude forms a base and foundation
allowing your strength to be ordained.

Your heart is your source of power
releasing the energy to ignite your inner fire,
Your success comes forth through faith
when your brain joins your heart's desire.

When David confronted the giant Goliath
he appeared as a small shepherd boy,
Yet he was most able to prove
that his slingshot was not a child's toy.

Your success is not dependent on your size
it depends on your inner wisdom,
Victory belongs to the winners
those that pour the fuel on their inner vision!

Telling Lies

A lie is an act of deception
with intent to contradict and corrupt,
The deceiver avoids the truth
with the lie being a coverup.

Most lies are told to protect
and to avoid presenting the facts,
To deny or place blame on another
by attempting to avoid further attacks.

Telling lies means to hide behind a mask
with statements that twist right to wrong,
By misguiding and contradicting what is right
the deceiver destroys life's truthful song.

Telling lies can develop into bad habits
with others losing confidence in you,
Discard all thoughts of dishonesty
and focus on your spirit of truth!

That Special Something

There is a special something
that knows what life is all about,
It beats to a constant rhythm
its mission it to love and give it out.

Its nature and its purpose
is essential to life itself,
Always active and always resting
like two bookends on a shelf.

Providing a background to life's music
as it powers itself along,
With its self-propelling engine always churning
tuning in to life's sweet music song.

At the center of its being
the Holy Spirit rests in peace,
No better place exists
than where the shepherd guards his sheep.

God keeps all things in His circle
so He can see all things inside,
Yet He needed to have a counterpart
to observe within and to forever abide.

This miracle of miracles
is God's lifegiving work of art,
It moves and works its magic
it is your loving human heart!

The Ark of the Covenant

The original spiritual spark of divinity
embedded in man's heart at creation,
Is a most sacred and holy thing
because it is protected with great devotion.

God established this central spark
placing it in man's heart as a holy covenant,
Where it could grow and prosper
igniting man's immortal development.

God's covenant is first contained in a sacred ark
to protect when placed in the most holy temple,
When the ark containing the covenant is removed
no spiritual unfoldment will man encounter.

Placed inside the ark were the two tablets of stone
where God made a covenant with the sons of Israel,
Known as the Ten Commandments revealed to Moses
containing God's sacred laws established for His people.

The ark belongs in Jerusalem
the heart's center of peace,
God's covenant is forever protected
so His love and devotion will never cease!

The Best is Yet to Come

What does it mean to promise?
and are promises only a token?
How can I know for certain?
that God's promises will not be broken?

A promise is a declaration of assurance
a pledge and an affirmation,
God's promises are His Word of honor
built on a firm foundation.

God wants you to be aware of His promises
His guarantee and commitment to never fail,
His promises are His sacred Word
and on His promises, you can set your sail.

God's laws were established in the beginning
and His kingdom will never end,
Man must believe God will fulfill His promises
so he can rejoice and forever transcend.

God promises the end of suffering
and victory over death will be won,
His promises, through Christ Jesus, are eternal
rest assured that the best is yet to come!

The Blessings of Each Day

Every morning God does grant us
another beautiful day,
We may not absorb its beauty
when our minds are far away.

We may encounter troubles
or we may be filled with joy,
Both can be a blessing
when our faith we do deploy.

God presents us with a challenge
with whatever comes our way,
By being content and truly thankful
to be alive for another day!

The Blood of Christ

The blood of Christ is a life-giving power
beyond intellectual comprehension,
A form of energy that far transcends
all inherent life-current plans of purification.

The potency in the blood of Christ
through spiritual principles in the Word of God,
Offers nothing less than purification of the mind
as God rules through the justice of His rod.

Blood represents life through the body
but is not life itself,
It is a spiritual principle
manifesting in mind as absolute wealth.

Through the purified spirit of Jesus
you and the Heavenly Father are sanctified,
In whose image and likeness, we are One
together with our hearts glorified!

The Butterfly

The butterfly is special and symbolizes new life
first a crawling caterpillar before receiving its wings,
Free and alive as it moves and floats through the air
no longer earth bound, new glory it brings.

The changes in life were planned that way
God knew that transition was the key to a new high,
First crawling then flying, then soaring to Heaven's sky
reminding us how our Lord Jesus showed the world how to fly.

Our Lord preaches and teaches
His creation well-planned at its birth,
His instructions are transforming
lifting you far above God's treasured green earth.

Each of us, like the butterfly
was created to rise and shine,
So we can join our loving Savior
and hear Him say "You Are Mine"!

The Collapse

A financial tsunami
is building a base,
Debt levels are rising
while accelerating the pace.

The financial empires
will be overwhelmed by the waves,
All will be affected
and most left in a daze.

This bubble is bursting
and there is nothing to replace,
The illusion that all is secure
will leave nothing to embrace.

Like a spark that ignites a forest fire
and clears the forest floor,
Man's self-made creation will collapse
and those remaining must rebuild once more.

A castle built on the sinking sand
cannot support man's lofty plans,
The bigger the structure, the weaker the sand
get ready for the tsunami as it heads for dry land!

The Courage to Enter In

Jesus spoke to those listening
that He has come that they may have life,
To have it more abundantly
when hearing His voice free of fear and strife.

Reach for the handle
and open the door,
Then enter into my Kingdom
where we can embrace and adore.

The keeper of the sheepfold
will never leave you or forsake you,
You are standing at the threshold
let your courage and love pull you through.

Your name is written in my Book of Life
a place for you has been set aside,
Your family and friends await you
and together will forever abide!

The Cross of Jesus

As I look up from the foot of Jesus
I behold the blood He shed,
He followed God's plan of perfection
so you and I could be eternally fed.

He gave up His life through sacrifice
so He could fulfill His Father's will,
Only through the power of God's amazing love
could He die on Calvary hill.

Jesus Christ is truly our Savior
His love and grace we could never erase,
His cross remains His enduring symbol
of how He died to save the human race!

The Domain of Change

Change is inevitable
and its movement is fast,
Change rushes down the mountain
carrying with it all the past.

Change marches forward
and it never looks back,
The only thing it knows
is to stay on the fast track.

Change can be beneficial
yet it won't remain to be seen,
It will not stop and ponder
to review the last scene.

Change doesn't listen
it does its own thing,
You can't contain it or restrain it
it knows not how to cling.

Change won't allow you
to hold back or regress,
Yet change itself is unchanging
unlike all the rest!

The Freedom to Choose

A gift from your heavenly Father
A sign of trust and unending love,
The freedom to choose the path you'll follow
Granted by decree from up above.

In His image God has made you
Without limitations He sees you complete,
No restrictions were planted within you
You are free to choose and avoid defeat.

God rules with laws and principles
With truth, they withstand the test of time,
Forming a background of love in action
A foundation securing the branch to the vine.

God's vision is beyond man's comprehension
Only He could demonstrate life on earth,
Descending from heaven's glory and compassion
He sent His Son to teach us from His birth.

Right choice is God's divine blessing
Giving man the wisdom to conform to His Son,
Returning to man's home base in heaven
Allows man's choice to ensure victory will be won!

The Genius of the Seed

At the center of all life
is the reproductive seed,
Its destiny is to become
exactly what God designed it to be.

For a seed to grow and prosper
it must be placed in holy ground,
Where it can produce a harvest
allowing itself to abound.

The seed you sow
connects to God's supply,
His Word has been established
on His truth, you can rely.

Inside every seed
is the Word of God,
Each man is a seed of genius
springing forth from God's fertile sod.

Life itself is self-sustaining
as it reproduces its only kind,
When its image is revealed to be
exactly what God had in mind!

The Gift of Grace

Grace is for believers
which is given by the Lord,
Blessing those who trust Him
He who protects with His flaming sword.

From the source of pure love and compassion
sufficient to bring forth fresh new life,
Extended to the faithful
to fulfill His heart's delight.

Love must express and flow most freely
and release its power and grace,
So God's children can behold
their Lord's beloved and glorious face!

The Golden Rule

There is a rule that's golden
that most men are not inclined,
It declares that man must treat others
as themselves to be refined.

This rule of life is essential
if man is to live in peace,
To live "in Christ" is fundamental
and all opposition among mankind must cease.

Cooperation must become a priority
for as you give you shall receive,
By applying the golden rule
you'll discover the power when you believe!

The Golden Seed

Within each and every man
God planted a golden seed,
With infinite power and possibility
He gave each man all he would ever need.

The golden seed He planted
was a mind just like His own,
Full of wisdom, truth and love
capable of rolling away a troublesome stone.

When you stop thinking about your troubles
and think about God instead,
The trouble, whatever it is,
will soon be gone and can no longer be fed.

There is not much more to the process
God made it simple to do,
Let you mind continuously think about God
over and over let Him come through.

By repeating a statement of absolute truth
such as "God and I are One",
The golden seed God planted in your mind
assures your troubles are gone and victory is won!

The Great Liberator

As a child of the "Most High"
we are lower than God and His angels,
We are the key part of His creation
depending on Him to guard us from dangers.

Since God is high and lifted up
man must rise up to reach the higher side,
Without a way across the wide gap between us
we need a bridge to cross over the great divide.

God provided the bridge to cross over
designed when His plan was first conceived,
Knowing man's sin would separate us from Him
His Son came to bridge the gap for those who believed.

God loves His children dearly
He infused them with love and purity,
His home belongs to His believers
He must liberate them to return home for eternity!

The Heart and the Mind

The mind loves the heart
and the heart loves the mind,
Functioning together as brothers
they are a glorious blessing to mankind.

Guiding, sustaining, and protecting at all times
the heart and the mind are truly divine,
Essential to life itself
they fuse the branch to the vine.

The mind is a servant
worshiping the heart as the king,
All glory and honor
to the king we will bring.

The heart is a sanctuary
created direct from our Father's design,
Working in concert with all God's children
to transform and resurrect each and every mind.

With the rhythm of our heartbeats
enhancing our voices to rise and sing,
With all joy and praise
we worship Jesus Christ, our Savior and our King!

The Heartbeat of the Soul

Music is the heartbeat of the soul
God's tune so man can adapt and move along,
From the top of a mountain to the valley below
God will forever be singing His song.

Music is God's healing message
allowing man's mind to tune-in to the heart,
Lifting your spirits upwards
and relaxing life's stops and starts.

Music relieves man from pressure
and causes your feet to want to prance,
The energy coming from the heart's music
tells you to grab a partner and dance.

Man needs to listen to the music
to control the heartbeat of his soul,
His mind and heart maintain life's rhythm
and adjust to life's rock and roll.

To lift or to comfort life's comings
man must listen to music's full scale,
Stay calm, cool, and collected
lift anchor and get ready to sail.

From the tunes that lift us to the mountain top
to the ballads that comfort and console,
God's songs will always be playing
so man can move forward on his stroll!

The Highwaymen

They were known as the Highwaymen
Waylon, Willie, Johnny and Kris,
Releasing their talents
entertaining with a kiss.

Individual legends
in both lyrics and notes,
Blending together
life's stories they wrote.

With the rhythm of guitar strings
and the heartbeat of the soul,
Entertaining God's children
was their mission and role.

Loving God and country
they traveled state to state,
Singing songs of gladness
marching on toward Heaven's gate.

Brothers on life's highway
connected with a song,
Living on forever
in our memories where they belong!

The Human Body

All parts of the human body
are inner connected and a part of the whole,
Each part has a purpose
designed to work together with a common goal.

When one part becomes dysfunctional
or refuses to join the body's team,
Other parts are impacted
and become unable to fulfill God's dream.

There is a part of the body
that can diagnose and control,
The human mind is a gift from Heaven
to defend and protect the soul.

Your mind must remain alert
and it must never be dismissed,
Listening to the rhythm of your heartbeat
it will be met with a holy kiss.

The mind has power to fuel its existence
which is sourced within the human soul,
Through the gift of the Holy Spirit
each part of the body can forever remain whole.

Life itself has many facets
and divided it cannot be sustained,
To function as our Creator intended
we must honor and bless what He ordained!

The Importance of Small

Do little things matter?
Are small steps essential to success?
Can you skip past the small steps?
And still accomplish your intent to do your best?

Little things do matter
Each recipe requires parts of exact amounts,
By changing or leaving out the details
Requires a restart so you can complete and surmount.

The structure of all things includes many pieces
Each piece is an essential part of the whole,
By excluding any part of a structure
Causes the structure to collapse into a sinking hole.

Your body consists of numerous parts and pieces
And your mind must discover, organize and define,
Yet the controlling part that's essential to all the others
Is the purifying filter of your heart's divine design.

To avoid skipping past the small stuff
Relax and take needed time to digest,
It's the little things that truly matter
Slow down, review the details and do your best!

The Intuitive Wisdom of the Heart

The human heart was designed to control and prosper
its assignment was to keep alive and purify,
God programed the heart to apply love and all knowledge
so it could connect, fortify and glorify.

Wisdom is the main ingredient in know-how
and both knowledge and skill are the keys to victory,
The heart knows how to connect and communicate
as the brain stores up the keys to everlasting liberty.

The heart has the courage and the ability
to take action and be ready to defend,
It is prepared to protect against every challenge
and on its ability and faith you can depend.

The heart is a vital force in life's extension
true wisdom is etched in every beat,
Its power and intuition are stronger than any other
it allows no other to take its front row seat!

The Key to Happiness

You must accentuate the positive
and eliminate the negative,
Say the lyrics to a popular song
advising to latch on to the affirmative.

To spread joy to the maximum
and find the door to happiness,
Accentuate the positive
and eliminate all the rest.

When everything looks dark
and you know not what you should do,
Just accentuate the positive
so the negative can't break through.

Your mind adores the positive
and enjoys what will accrue,
When you accentuate the positive
and let the negative say "adieu"!

The Lord's Prayer

There is a special program
that man must claim and swallow,
Set forth by our Lord and Savior
for man to apply and follow.

The program He taught us
is in our Father's perfect design,
His loving and caring prayer
blessing all he calls "mankind".

Straight forward and concise
allowing man to comprehend,
Guaranteed and promised
teaching man to understand.

Our Lord's intended purpose
is to teach and to convey,
The truth of His creation
encouraging man to follow and obey.

Listen to His message
absorb the truth within,
Follow where He guides you
rejoice and commence to win!

The Love of Giving

From the act of giving
comes the ability to receive,
Giving is a heartfelt experience
lifting both hearts to believe.

Receiving without giving
means a fear leads one to hoard,
The excess that is not needed
won't flow out of a blocked front door.

Giving produces adrenalin
exciting and lifting the soul,
Nature abhors a vacuum
and must fill up an empty hole.

Giving is a repetitious habit
when learning it's others you embrace,
Receiving back what you are giving
is not the motive that blesses your case.

Giving is a gracious act of loving
without expectation of return,
Blessing both giver and receiver
relieving the need for further concern!

The Magic of the Sun

There is a ball of fire
shining down from its Heavenly tower,
The sustainer of life...its warmth our delight
the source of everlasting power.

Our Creator placed the sun in the heavens
to shine its bright light on mankind,
With its power and its might...leading man to the light
the key to connecting the branch to the vine.

The sun is a magical reminder
of the only true source of delight,
When God sent His only son...assuring man's victory be won
reflecting the full glory of His bright shining light!

The Majesty of the Heart

In each human being
God placed His precious heart,
In control from the beginning
Until death do us part.

All other bodily organs
Depend on each heartbeat,
The heart is at the center
The power source from God's love seat.

The heart has a dual purpose
Guarding both the body and the soul,
One is physical and the other is spiritual
Designed to sustain and make man whole.

Our Creative Father
Knew His heart could wipe out sin,
So, He placed it in man's center
Where His Holy Spirit's love could thrive and win!

The Mirror of My Mind

My mind is like a mirror
reflecting back a perfect view,
With no reason to change the image
for any change is up to you.

If you wonder about your image
or don't like what reflects back to you,
Any change you wish to make
will reflect straight back into your view.

What you are is what you'll see
exactly what you were meant to be,
What goes in must come out
your image is what you're all about.

Reflections cannot change what is in the mirror's view
they can only reflect back what comes shining through,
The mirror tells the story of man's amazing mind
it absorbs and repeats what is clearly defined!

The National Pastime

The game is now starting
with nine innings to play,
Both teams are prepared and ready
on this bright and sunny day.

The umpires are in position
the pitcher has the ball,
His windup is now in motion
the plate umpire will make the call.

The batter adjusts his helmet
his feet now nearing the plate,
His eyes are on the pitcher
and his swing must not be early or late.

The catcher tells the pitcher
to throw a fast ball or a curve,
The batter awaits the fast-moving target
telling his bat to hit what is served.

Each game consists of strikeouts
extra bases and pop-ups won,
The team that claims the victory
is the one scoring the winning run.

If the pitcher loses confidence
and loses control of his belief,
The bullpen comes to the rescue
and provides the manager some relief.

A baseball game can be relaxing
or can excite and test your nerve,
Like life itself tells a story
and delivers the score you truly deserve!

The Open Door

The secret of happiness
is just beyond the magic door,
This door is not just hidden
it is discovered by those Christ does adore.

To enter through the doorway
you must be eager to enter in,
For the glory you will encounter
will erase and forgive your every sin.

The map to find this doorway
you are holding in your hand,
Containing the complete instructions
His Word holds the key to the promised land.

If your desire is to see this doorway
and be invited to pass on through,
You must love your Lord and Savior
just like He loves and blesses you!

The Perfect Image of the Heart

The human heart
was imaged by the Lord,
It had to be perfect
and accomplish what God adored.

It must be life-sustaining
with a continuous rhythm and beat,
While it loves and caresses
from God's forgiving mercy seat.

God designed the human heart
to be a cleansing filter for blood flow,
And it had to be a dwelling place
as a home for His Holy Spirit's soul.

The heart is central to creation
other parts depending on blood's flow,
God took His perfect image
and blessed it as His best of show.

God programmed the human heart
to function on its own,
Itself a gift from Heaven's Kingdom
sent from God's abiding throne!

The Perfect View

Do you feel empty?
disappointed and under stress?
Uncertain about your future?
needing more than just a guess?

We must model the characteristics of our Creator
He designed us to follow through,
That's the way He works
so just listen and start anew.

Life is meant to be celebrated
lock it in and don't look back,
Only God can fulfill a human heart
He's the only one who can provide what you lack.

Two sides of life are available
and the choice is up to you,
Listen then lock in God's presence
and claim His perfect view!

The Power of Faith

Faith is not what you do
faith is what you are,
Faith is your entry to power
faith is your best stronghold by far.

Faith comes forth when you're tested
and is established when you're on trial,
Your faith will produce your freedom
faith allows you to go the extra mile.

Faith precedes all solutions
faith rests when not in use,
Faith contains all the ingredients
to produce God's amazing truth.

Faith triggers your inner power
and follows your mind's belief,
To put your faith in motion
just believe and watch it bring relief.

So, faith comes by hearing
and hearing by the Word of God,
Listen and keep your ears clear and open
then clap your hands and commence to applaud!

The Power of Love

True love is unconditional
you were created to be loved and to give love,
Man must hate sin and love the sinner
circumstances must not prevent us from rising above.

God loves every single person
no matter what their sin may be,
God extends His care and mercy
to those who want to be set free.

God keeps no record of wrongs
as He loves without limitations,
Whoever believes in God's love
will be received without conditions.

God considers bad behavior worth correcting
for all His children make mistakes,
Love has the full power to erase and embrace
as God extends His gift of amazing grace!

The Power of Two

It takes at least two
to even have a chance,
It takes two to tango
to make it to the dance.

With two you can multiply
bearing fruit by the score,
Going alone won't work
and you can't open the golden door.

Your mind must learn to focus
and picture clearly what you seek,
Without focus you will discover
you will soon be up the creek.

The seeds you plant for harvest
must be sprinkled with all your faith,
While you listen to your inner mentor
your partner who with you will wait.

On your journey to reach the target
problems may divert and make you late,
Yet they are instructions to assist you
so you can cross over through Heaven's gate!

The Power of Words

The word "awesome"
is a word to use with caution,
This breathtaking word is so amazing
no definition fully describes "awesome".

They say the appropriate definition
is "wonderful" and "overwhelming",
Some say "magnificent" and "stupendous"
while others describe it as "mind-blowing".

My son-in-law adds a word ahead of it
and the word he adds is "totally",
To be fully aware of the power of "awesome"
just add "totally" to complete its full majesty.

To combine two words together
provides a power not soon forgotten,
You gain power and impact when you combine them
and proclaim that something is "totally awesome"!

When the day comes and I arrive in Heaven
and see the New World in every blossom,
I know that King Solomon in all his glory and splendor
would lift his voice and shout out "totally awesome"!

The Power to Heal

There is a place inside
where only God can go,
This place is sacred
and only God can know.

Inside is God's home base
it's where He lives and dwells,
The power of His Holy Spirit
transforms and truly heals.

The key that will unlock
the door to the heart and soul,
Requires faith to gain entry
where His power can make you whole.

With God's love at the center
and your heart prepared to embrace,
Your healing is accomplished
as God's love sets the pace!

The Purpose of Satan

Is Satan the personification of evil?
or is Satan the truth exposing our Savior's soul?
When I was young and without experience
I relied on what my emotions foretold.

To see God in all of his glory
you must know Him from all sides and both ends,
God's image He placed in all His children
distinguishes life from both the outside and from within.

Almighty God is both alpha and omega
He's the start and stop of man's concept of time,
God is both the subject and the verb of all activity
since He formed and created His song that rhymes.

God created the light that exposes the darkness
His Word teaches and contrasts right from wrong,
God made both ends of life's equation
So man could count his blessings
while singing God's marching song!

The Revelation

In the book of The Revelation
Christ revealed things that will soon take place,
A beast will assume his authority
and place his mark on the human race.

Placing a mark on their right hand or forehead
to identify and control with his tricks,
For he is the number of man
and his number is six, six, six.

The number six represents the temporal man
God made him on day number six,
Three represents the domain of the Holy Trinity
where man chooses the power of his picks.

The evil beast in man is self-serving
with intent to rule in absolute control,
Disobedience will not be tolerated
his fellowman cannot survive in Satan's hole.

Man must look inside for strength and courage
with minds focused on steering the drifting ship,
Many others depend on the captain's guidance
knowing Jesus Christ controls with the firmest grip!

The Spirit Within

The spirit within you
is reverent and pure,
God made you to perfection
to last and endure.

He assigned you a mission
you must discover and claim,
Drawing you to His heart
to be a member of His team.

Uniquely made each one of you are
by God's divine and creative laws,
Blessed with perfect beauty
and made without any flaws.

His instructions are learned
from His story found in His Word,
To guide you to your home in Heaven
from the lessons you read and heard.

God is your Master
your Creator and King,
He is the One and the Only
to make your heart sing,

God will be with you
with His love that won't cease,
Your partner in His Kingdom
as He brings forth His peace!

The Stillness of the Mind

The mind becomes creative
when thought is gone and all is still,
Its real power is awakened
to accomplish what it will.

Inner stillness gives form
to the creative nature from within,
Man's thoughts cannot interfere
set aside so new life can begin.

When in the stillness
and the mind is put to rest,
Amazing things can happen
as you are free to do your best.

The key to joy and happiness
is when your thoughts have lost control,
Freeing your mind from all distractions
as you lift your precious soul!

The Story of David

The Holy Bible is at the pinnacle of all teaching
God's story of His truth comes into full view,
Like the story of the love of David who transgressed
yet returned back home, like me and you.

David was a young shepherd
who watched over the sheep night and day,
He worshipped the Lord almighty
and sought each lamb that had gone astray.

Later on, he must face the giant Goliath
who stood tall and massive all alone,
Unafraid David stood up against the giant
and slayed him with just a single stone.

David became the first ruler of both Israel and Judah
after king Saul died and David later became the king,
With David 's skills as both a warrior and writer of psalms
he ruled for 33 more years, showing what love could bring.

One night David beheld beautiful Bathsheba
from his palace roof he saw her bathing in all her glory,
David lost control of his spirit's center
and thus began a new direction in his story.

David ordered Bathsheba's husband, Uriah
to enter a dangerous battlefield,
So he would not safely return back home
and he would shortly be killed.

The Story of David (continued)

David then took Bathsheba as his wife
and then realized what he had done,
He had disobeyed his God and Maker
for he had sinned and no victory had been won.

His righteousness took hold and overwhelmed him
seeking his loving Father, he found Him,
Waiting with His arms wide open
receiving him back into His kingdom within.

Bathsheba gave birth to a baby boy
who would later become the ruling king,
King Solomon was wise with power and dominion
who knew the songs he must sing.

David communed with God in his youth
he closely reflected divine love,
When he developed his human characteristics
he manifested human limitations, not from above.

The heart is at the center through which spirit rules
and David represents God's beloved,
God is love and His kingdom is within you
it is where you can believe and dream of.

David's life is a prelude to Christ's coming
as God communicates the truth He foretold,
Each child is God's heart manifesting
as we rejoice and let our love unfold!

The Testing Ground

The world is at my fingertips
it's at my beck and call,
Yet the world is not my future
it's where I'll rise or fall.

The world is where I'm tested
it's where I attend class to educate,
The world is not my playground
it's where I'll graduate.

The world is not my destination
it's a stop along life's way,
I must travel on the earthly side
and enter the gate to a brighter day.

God designed and assigned my homework
in the world where I was born,
He placed me in His marching band
and taught me to toot His horn.

God taught me to take the small steps
and to walk before I run,
Then He placed His Holy Spirit inside my heart
and introduced me to His Son!

The Tree of Life

The life of all creation
is like a mighty tree,
First a seed about to blossom
for all the world to see.

With its roots firmly planted
to support the many branches it will display,
Coming into being
what God ignites each glorious day.

As it grows and prospers
reaching into Heaven's sky,
The birds rest in its branches
supporting wings that soar and fly.

With water to sustain it
and power from the brightest sun,
Ripe fruit will be its blessing
until all is said and done.

An extension of itself
and expressing what is meant to be,
Behold pure love in motion
becoming the joy that is truly free.

When storms arrive and threaten
it firmly stands up tall,
As it hears the winds of mercy
and absorbs the spirit's call.

The tree of life is connected
to a forest so refined,
With branches kissing one another
reaching out with pure love in mind!

The Truth About Time

Time is divided in sections
which are created solely by man,
From the viewpoint of spirit
time cannot be seen like grains of sand.

Divisions of time reveal a process
Which signifies God's law of progression,
Progress is achieved when understanding
climbs the ladder of manifestation.

Man believes that time is a reality
and that eternity is an endless period of time,
Things that are spiritual and eternal
cannot be measured with ticks and chimes.

In the world outside we live in
it's a good habit to be punctual and on time,
Best your thoughts not be hurried
stay calm and declare that all is fine!

The Way They Were

My mother and father were important to me
they both loved me without end,
My brother, sister and I were blessed
by parents who taught us to be best friends.

We experienced life together
and we functioned as a team,
We spent much time together
my parents shared a special dream.

Both mom and dad were teachers
and put forth their loving hand,
They lived their lives as examples
knowing Christ Jesus was the way to stand.

Although they both have departed
their presence is close by to stay,
I will cherish them both forever
as their love taught me how to pray!

Thirsty

Like a drop of water
can quench my thirst,
Only you O Lord
must I seek first.

Your righteousness will satisfy
when in a desert storm,
Your forgiving grace and mercy
guides me to be reborn.

With your Holy Spirit inside me
I am never all alone,
Your love is transferring to pure water
a lifeless rock or stone.

Dear Lord I need your presence
I need you every hour,
I need to drink your water
like a beautiful fragrant flower.

For your love and tender mercy
I sing out my thanks and praise,
For your righteous gifts of joy, I drink
I will bless you for all my days!

Thou Shall Not Kill

I am a human being
formed in the image of Almighty God, alone,
My Creator sent forth His commandments
and carved them on two tablets of stone.

The sixth of God's Ten Commandments
declares that "You shall not murder",
This does not refer to killing in general, but to
premeditated murder of one person by another.

God reproduces His offspring
by His design implanted in the seed,
When man implants his seed in a woman
God's heart instructs man not to destroy or impede.

The boundaries around an individual's life are sacred
and the unborn child man must guard and protect,
Your God is the supplier of all your needs
and even an unborn child you must not reject.

God's authority does not require man's interpretation
and man's legal decisions do not supersede God's demands,
God loves each and every child He creates
and abortion violates God's sixth command!

To Be

"To Be" means to become
what your dreams say you should be,
Things your inner voice whispers
while the Holy Spirit issues its decree.

Your outer self must follow
what your inner voice beckons you to be,
Your future is within your grasp
with open arms to welcome thee.

The song you sing is sacred
as it brings the truth into view,
Guiding you to reach the Kingdom
where with open arms God embraces you.

The bridge you must cross over
will lead you to victory,
As you reach your destination
and become what you were born to be!

Together as One

The one "Mind", or Intelligence, of the universe
is God's "Spirit", known as "Mind",
God, the "Father", is "Mind" in principle
the source of manifestation of every kind.

God the "Father" is "Being" in the absolute
with unlimited supply in store,
His power and trust are available
both now and forever more.

The "Son" is the "I Am" identity
revealed in God's creative plan,
Present to accomplish each assignment
assisting in every way He can.

The "Holy Spirit" is God's personality of "Being"
breathing forth the fullness of Christ, the "Son",
All together, they are God's law in action
functioning in harmony and truly as "One"!

Trapped in Adversity

When we experience intense adversity
we typically focus on momentary trouble,
Failing to see any beneficial value
while suffering through the rubble.

However, God has a specific purpose
for the hardships we encounter,
His desire is to teach us to hate evil
even though we continue to allow it to fester.

God knows the world is permeated by evil
and it cannot be avoided at all times,
We must remove ourselves from temptations
to prevent being trapped in the world's crimes.

The Heavenly Father can comfort and advise you
by teaching you to recognize evil's ways,
Pray and ask Him to shield and guard you
so you can overcome the traps that evil lays!

Trust and Believe

Your assignment as a Christian believer
is much more than you are open to receive,
You may hesitate to allow faith and trust
to fully focus on the Lord and believe.

You must keep your mind centered on God's Word
to develop and expand your trust,
So the promises that are disclosed from the Scriptures
are alive and become more than a handful of dust.

The key to remain secure and steady
and know that all is well,
Is to choose the Lord Jesus as your Savior
and invite His Holy Spirit into your heart to dwell.

Why dig deep to discover the treasure,
with the pick and shovel at your command?
When the truth that you are seeking
is already in the palm of your hand!

Uniquely Made

By observing God's creation
you'll discover no duplicates of any kind,
Each individual creation
is unique in God's imaged design.

Although He created species
and formed branches connected and aligned,
Each unit birthed from the inside core
was different and uniquely one of a kind.

With a closer look at human beings
no two have fingerprints alike,
Each voice, each face, and each mind
are uniquely similar and reflect God's holy light.

God's creation is formed in a circle
embracing all He formed on the inside,
His world spins and encircles all He created
so His love would forever abide!

United as One

One with the Father
One with the Son,
One with the Holy Spirit
United as One.

Walking together
Forever at peace,
Loving each other
Never to cease.

Living together
Helping each other,
Lifting our neighbor
Needing a big brother.

Our spirits are united
In tune with Father and Son,
Our hearts embracing each other
With the Holy Spirit, as One!

Unity of Spirit

Today my companion and soulmate
left me to return back home,
Leaving me and entering the gates of glory
finding peace under God's golden dome.

Our souls were connected in purpose
our love for each other was refined,
Our legacy to one another
was to bless and be aligned.

The time we were joined together
we moved forward step by step,
Now gone but not forgotten
as I recall how I was blessed.

My continued journey along life's highway
we will join together hand in hand,
Always one in mind and spirit
marching forward to the Promised Land!

Use Your Talents

When God first imagined your being
He gave you a unique set of skills,
His plan was for you to deploy them
no matter how high the steep hills.

You possess talents uniquely your own
able to achieve levels as if only a dream,
Your assignment is to cross over the goal line
as a member of God's winning team.

To develop your talents to a high level
you must practice and practice some more,
Knowing that desire and determination
brings forth the goals you earnestly explore.

God's desire is for you to be successful
and accomplish much more than you perceive,
God's strength and might will support you
that's why He gave you the talents to succeed!

Utopia

God imaged a world of perfection
a world we call the utopia connection,
As He prepared to release His imagination
He added a final piece to His divine commission.

God knew that His plan must include evolution
and the truth requires man's devotion,
He added free will to complete the equation
so man could choose and make his own decision.

The living world described as God's creation
is far beyond man's comprehension,
To adapt man must learn to employ relaxation
so he can choose confession to achieve salvation.

God offers the true source of education
with the truth conveyed without negative emotion,
His light shines through the darkest dimension
bringing hope to man's fear and the world's commotion!

Vision

Vision is the ability
to see what lies up ahead,
With intent and a focused mindset
you will clearly see where you are led.

Vision sees beyond the horizon
with understanding as its goal,
It can encircle a moving target
and view it from pole to pole.

All advancement thrives with practice
and determination leads the pack,
Maintain an attitude of gratitude
for there is nothing you will lack.

Your vision will empower you
to take hold of God's outstretched hand,
Where no fear can overwhelm you
as your vision is at your command!

Warm Bright Sunshine

Spring is here
it's in the air and I'm fully aware,
The days seem longer
the bright, sunny days are here.

When I look up
and lift up my face,
I feel the warm, bright sun
blessing me with Christ's healing grace.

New days are arriving
as the sun begins its descent,
Its bright light shines upon me
showing God's love is always present.

God's love is amazing
expressing its glorious light,
Shining and healing
His love clearly in sight!

What's Wrong?

The sanctity of life
is God's gift and blessing to man,
He loves each of His children
He wants man to protect all His clan.

Man has chosen to kill
an innocent unborn child in the womb,
To sell the child's body parts
before tossing the remains in a tomb.

The innocent child
awaits its first breath,
While the forces of evil
execute the child's death.

We send aid and assistance
to extend the lives of foreign souls,
While we turn the other cheek at home
and toss our children in dark holes.

We allow illegal immigrants
to flood through our front doors,
While we destroy our unborn infants
proving we don't love and adore.

What's wrong with this picture?
Have we gone totally mad?
God must be crying and weeping
I'm sure He's not laughing and glad.

What's wrong with this picture?
in our land of the free,
God's anger is building
just you wait and see!

Where is Jesus?

Where is Jesus?
and how can I find Him?
Open my eyes so I can see
and let His grace release me from sin.

Jesus is never where you believe
He ought to be,
He's on a schedule
He hears you and understands your plea.

He wasn't with Lazarus
when he got sick and died,
He wasn't in His own tomb
when the women went there and cried.

Jesus is always busy
His Holy Spirit is awake both day and night,
With His mind focused on your well-being
He is sending forth His resurrecting light.

His home abides within you
and He surely can be found,
Just close your eyes and see Him
you and He are standing on Holy Ground!

Where Joy Abides

Joy comes from the Lord
where He lives and dwells inside of you,
Joy emerges from the inside out
where the Lord sees the perfect view.

Joy is the seed of happiness
and knows how to bless and sing,
Bursting forth through the walls of darkness
with a song that only a joyous heart can bring.

Joy cannot stay hidden
it breaks free to bless the soul,
Joy cannot be contained
for releasing love is its main goal.

Joy is a descendant of the truth
it embraces what it adores,
It spreads itself around you
when it releases itself, it pours!

Where the Holy Spirit Dwells

The Holy Spirit is my facilitator
the One who enables my continuous life flow,
His indwelling presence fulfills His promise
to energize my heart and soul.

The choice to connect to His power
He gave to you and me,
The door to the Kingdom of Heaven is open
so believers can be set free.

The Holy Spirit dwells within me
to lift me up to where I belong,
As a member of His choir
I let His voice become my song.

The Holy Spirt aligns with my spirit
our loving spirits unite as One,
His Word declares His promise
so I can live together with my Father and Son.

As my journey of life continues
I will squeeze His hand tightly in mine,
Knowing that His will and purpose
is to unite my branch with His everlasting vine!

Where You Are

Paradise is God's Holy ground
it exists right here, not far,
You don't have to seek it
it's right here, where you are.

You were born and placed
in God's garden of delight,
God knows you as His offspring
so He brought forth His perfect light.

Paradise is God's pleasure grounds
where the purity of mind begins to form,
Where the soul believes in the Almighty
allowing only good to be the norm.

The Word of God teaches about your Father
and how He placed His seed in you,
So you could dwell in Paradise, and He
could love and bless in Heaven's brightest blue.

Paradise is not a future place
or a reward for being good,
Paradise is right where you are
it's where God's pure love said He should.

Paradise is not a place where you go
after proving you passed some sort of test,
You are alive and standing on Holy ground
trust God, then let Him do the rest!

Where Your Treasure Lies

Your treasure lies over the horizon
and beneath your feet,
Waiting to be discovered
and exhibit its love so sweet.

As you move forth to greet it
it beckons to your heart's desire,
As it patiently awaits
with its all-consuming fire.

Your treasure lies in God's Heaven
uniquely designed for you alone,
Your faith and trust in God's abundance
leads you to your Father's most precious Son.

God promised you a blessing
designed with you in mind,
Placing your treasure so you would discover
God's gift inside your heart divine!

Who is the Greatest?

The disciples asked Jesus
"Who is the greatest in Heaven's Kingdom?"
Then Jesus replied with God's truth
and His pure and perfect wisdom.

In the world, your goal
is to ascend to the mountain top,
But first you must descend
and cause the spiral to come to a stop.

To enter the Kingdom of Heaven
you must cast off pride and self-majesty,
Jesus called forth one little child
who came forth because he believed in Me.

Life's purpose is to bring forth
love, happiness, and joy,
To do this you must have faith
believing that Christ is the One to employ.

The ones that enter the Kingdom
are the ones who are forgiven for their sins,
Those that believe in Christ's Holy Spirit
allow Christ to rise up and dwell within.

The greatest in the Kingdom
is not the one who seeks fortune and fame,
The chief ones among you
are those that believe in Christ's name!

Who We Are

Why is it hard to understand?
who you God, truly are?
Is it because we don't understand?
who we truly are?

God made us and sustained us
with a purpose, He refined,
His plan was to fulfill a promise
with love as the central design.

God blesses every child of His
each and every one,
He honored and expressed His amazing love
when he brought forth Jesus Christ, His Son.

You are a child of God our Father,
the One and only One,
His love is so amazing
when He declared it was finished
it was over and done.

As an extension of God's being
we are lifted beyond the highest star,
To a paradise set in Heaven
because of who we truly are!

Working in Concert

The organs of the human body
cannot function when all alone,
Being connected through a master network
with blood flowing from the heart's central zone.

The heart has long been viewed
as the center of thought, memory, and emotion,
More recently viewed as an isolated pump
the body's master organ.

In the rapidly changing world we live in
which is setting new records of speed,
Man is quickly becoming a roadblock
unable to understand or to lead.

From the rise in the employment of robots
to the creation of driverless cars,
Soon machines will direct all endeavors
and mankind will be living on Mars.

The human heart is an organ with many duties
tasked with purifying and pumping the body's blood,
It is also cleaning and filtering the brain's input
neither brain or the heart dragging the other through the mud.

The heart and brain are interconnected
in a partnership embracing each other with love,
The brain and heart analyzing all input
and together blessing the output from above!

Yes and No

Never say never
never say "No",
If you want to rise in the morning
you've got to get up and go.

"No" forces you backwards
back to the end of the line,
Say "Yes" when you greet the morning
so in the evening you can rest and recline.

Never doesn't mean to be fearful
and "No" doesn't mean to close the door,
Your spirit is your great up lifter
"Yes" means to get up off the floor!

Yesterday

Many thoughts have filtered
through my amazing mind,
My past has been exciting
many blessings did I find.

As I look back and ponder
the journey that got me here,
I count those many blessings
that I hold both near and dear.

The assignments I was given
have become a part of who I am,
The building blocks forming the foundation
supporting my desire to become a man.

The past escapes before you know it
and once gone it won't return,
Only in your memory bank
can you review and at best discern.

Soon you will discover
that yesterday is only a moment in time,
Here it comes and there it goes
give thanks that the past is mine.

Yesterday cannot be part of the present
its days have been put to rest,
You may visit the past from time to time
to remember where you built your nest!

You Are Invited

You are invited
to a very special place,
Unlike any other
full of love and Holy grace.

Many are invited
yet few will attend,
Those that pass through the doorway
will bask in glory without end.

A transformation process
will occur when you go inside,
There will be a radiant light
that will greet you and forever abide.

You'll connect to an infinite spirit
lifting you with all your precious charms,
Transporting you to a righteous paradise
as the Holy Spirit holds you in His loving arms.

Your invitation is extended
to bring you to a world of joy,
Back to the beginning
like a child with a brand new toy!

Your Creator's Love

Life is in motion
each raindrop to the river flows,
Each heartbeat sustains life
right down to your toes.

God created it all
and set it in motion,
With His guaranteed commitment
He extends His full devotion.

Each life is special
unique and divine,
You are destined for glory
God says "You are mine".

God's love and adoration
are truly the only one of its kind,
No other can compare
or try to outshine.

God is your true Father
He planted your seed,
Come let us worship
He will never mislead!

Your Dreams

Your future is determined
By what you dream about,
At rest your thoughts are energized
So you can eliminate any doubt.

You were born to live in happiness
And to find whatever you seek,
Your dreams are fuel to guide you
So you can reach your peak.

Dreams are nature's blessings
Designed with you in mind,
They surface when other thoughts are leaving
So you can remember what you find.

Dreams are God's solution
To lift you high and far,
So you can escape confinement
And release your genie from the jar!

Your Loving Father

Life without knowing your earthly father
one whose life force is planted in you,
Leaves a void beyond comprehension
a vacuum that the truth cannot undo.

When a vital ingredient is missing
not realizing what you do not possess,
The incomplete recipe you are made of
will forever be a roadblock to future success.

A loving father is a major key to life's foundation
a source of strength and abiding trust,
Each child needs a dedicated father
without him your life could be a bust.

No man can live without a father
for your true Father is alive within your heart,
The sooner you know how much He loves you
your life will enjoy a refreshing start!

Your Reflection

God's image is like a mirror
reflecting back what you are within,
What you see when looking in the mirror
is what God saw when your life first began.

You were made in God's loving image
so, He could see Himself in you,
You are the true apple of His eye
reflecting back Himself in a perfect view.

God's nature is to love and caress
He knows that life puts you to the test,
His Word teaches and explains
why you are one of His very best.

God's plan is to display life's full glory
in a world where man can choose,
His production is His life story
so you can love and never lose.

Take a good look in the mirror
and view yourself again,
You belong to your Almighty Creator
the One who lives within!

Zion

A fortified hill
a "holy hill" where David built his palace,
Where love abides with holy thoughts
clearly established as a spiritual fortress.

King David reflected God's divine love
so the heart, at the center of thought,
Would allow the Holy Spirit's ruling presence
to be secured with a golden knot.

God is love
allowing His kingdom "within you" to sing,
Where you can experience spiritual anointing
and love can rule as king.

The place where David built his palace
represented David's city of strong emotion,
Which later became a part of Jerusalem
the "New City" of God's abiding devotion!

Do You Really Believe?

As a believer in the profound teachings of Jesus Christ, I am troubled by the general lack of depth in the understanding and faith in the teachings of our Lord and Savior. In a world of prosperity and abundance man tends to embrace the many temptations and diversions which continuously entice his mind and his desire for earthly pleasure. Therefore, we must learn to know God---Spirit---as Mind, the one Mind or Intelligence of the universe. The manifestation of all that exists has its source in Mind. God, the Father, is Being in the absolute or Principle. As man's mind conceives an idea, this idea is the Son. The Holy Spirit is the law of God in action carrying out the creative plan. Man must be transformed by a renewing of the mind and must deny the existence of the "Old Man" and become the "New Man" where he can accept his inheritance as a child of God. Until man chooses the right path he will continue to live in the sensations of the flesh in which he places his trust. Man spends most of his time thinking about earthly matters and far too little time in dialog with the indwelling Christ. Experience is the best teacher and through relaxation and prayer man can seek and find a loving Father, his creative Son and experience the activity of the Holy Spirit.

Jesus taught us the truth saying:

"*I AM* the bread of life; he who cometh to Me shall never hunger; and he that believeth on Me shall never thirst." John 6:35

DO YOU REALLY BELIEVE?

"*I AM* the good shepherd; the good shepherd giveth his life for the sheep." John 10:11

DO YOU REALLY BELIEVE?

"*I AM* the way, the truth, and the life; no man cometh unto the Father but by Me." John 14:6

DO YOU REALLY BELIEVE?

"*I AM* the true vine, and my Father is the vinedresser." John 15:1

DO YOU REALLY BELIEVE?

"*I AM* the light of the world; he who follows Me shall not walk in darkness, but shall have the Light of life." John 8:12

DO YOU REALLY BELIEVE?

"*I AM* the door; by Me if any man enter in, he shall be saved, and shall go in and out, and find pasture." John 10:9

DO YOU REALLY BELIEVE?

"*I AM* the resurrection and the life; he who believes in Me shall live even if he dies." John 11:25

Jesus did not teach us anything we cannot do. His question is "Do you believe?", and through affirmation "According to your faith be it done to you." With Love all things are possible....God is Love and Love is the fulfilling of the law.

Our belief system, if based on false assumptions, prevents us from advancing into the truth of God's creation and all but locks us in to continue in our unsustainable thought mode. Man likes to believe that the manifest world is the source of all that is and through ignorance and self-serving desire finds himself off-track and heading in the wrong direction.

Two of my favorite Scripture passages are from Romans 13:12 and II Corinthians 5:17 where Paul states:

"The night is far spent, the day is at hand: let us therefore cast off the works of darkness, and let us put on the armor of light." "Therefore, if any man be in Christ, he is a new creation: old things are passed away; behold, all things have become new."

The best time for us to begin or to expand the transforming process is "Now". If not "Now", when?

In the strong name of Jesus, the Christ!

James P. Robson

Anxiety

After observing and loving each of my children over their lifetimes and after realizing that each of them are unique and special in ways of their own, I have experienced times when I wanted to intercede and bless them with some sort of gift or blessing that would make all struggles disappear and possibly make their lives easier or elevate them to some sort of effortless state. In an interview with actor Kirk Douglas in Esquire magazine in April 2001 at his then age of 84, he stated in various comments about what he had learned: "Give your children lots of rope. Allow them to make their own mistakes. Don't give them too much advice. Each child is different; you have to respect that. It's a crapshoot: You roll the dice, and you see what happens." My message is not intended to be a critique or a behavioral guideline but heartfelt comments which may be beneficial or worthy of consideration. I love each of my children with my full capability and as best I perceive my abilities and my understanding of their abilities and needs. Further, I feel my responsibility to safeguard myself through my behavior, my stewardship of the blessings that God has entrusted me with, and my health so that I can complete my mission to serve my God and to live a full and joyful life. I know that I must be true to myself and that the Lord helps those that help themselves. Self-sufficiency is essential in adult and family leadership and strong and self-sacrificial management and controls are required to rule the day. When any of your children struggle and you sense an urge to run to their rescue, you may be off base and confusing concern for love. The struggling child, to find true and lasting solutions, requires self-searching and must understand and acknowledge that they must participate in implementing changes in habits. Tough love is not always easy to apply but it must be the solution to avoid further anxiety and confusion. I am proud of each of my children and my desire is for them to discover and enjoy the basics of life with love as the central theme.

I am offering the following thoughts for consideration since over my lifetime I have been confronted with obstacles of various kinds including both the emotional and the financial variety. When circumstances occur, I have always tried to draw on my intellect and experience by considering my alternatives and solutions without the aid of others. I believe this is normal behavior and what most of us do as we want to stand on our own feet and we want others to know we are strong and self-sufficient. Pride is a most important virtue but it can also stand in our way if we don't come to the realization that we are all sinners and we all make mistakes. Therefore, we all need a place to turn to where we know for certain that we are forgiven for our shortcomings and we are loved beyond all we can hope for or even imagine. Fortunately, I have discovered that God's unwavering love for me and the presence of the Holy

Spirit, which lives within me and which was given as a legacy by the death of Jesus Christ on the cross, is available to me on a continuous basis. By knowing and claiming this ability to converse with the Almighty, I have found comfort and counsel for all my needs. Since I know this to be true, I want others, and surely my own children, to experience what I have discovered and what I wish to be a blessing to them as well. I tell myself this truth; that without God in my life I am incomplete and lost and with God I am blessed, whole, healthy and prosperous.

Over the years, I have also discovered that wisdom comes with experience as this is part of God's plan for us. To advance in knowledge and wisdom we must experience activity and be placed in conditions where we must sink or swim. God's plan is to put us to the test and see if we can apply our instilled talents and our discernment to figure things out for ourselves. God knew in advance that we would have failure and we would be diverted away from his guidance and instructions. This plan for us was intentional and for our own good so he could facilitate our growth and understanding to be more like him and so we could accomplish his will through our energy and focus. God wants to have dialog with us and so he speaks to us through our prayers and chats with him and through the various assignments he presents for us throughout our earthly existence. What happens in our lives is not just coincidence but God's way of getting our attention so we can advance and be an effective part of his special team. Man's problem is related to his listening skills being somewhat dormant and his lack of effort in staying in touch with his teacher, guide, mentor and Savior. In other words, he doesn't do his homework, skips school, and eventually drops out in favor of the temptations of the flesh.

What does God have to say about anxiety? Wrong choices can put you in a deeper state of anxiety. They have brought it on themselves. The medical profession says that persons continuously impacted with anxiety can have numerous health issues. When anxious you become tense and you don't know how to deal with it.

In Philippians 4: 4-7, Paul the Apostle says:

"Rejoice in the Lord always. Again, I say, rejoice! Let your gentleness be known to all men. The Lord is at hand. Be *anxious* for nothing, but in everything by prayer and supplication, with thanksgiving, let your requests be known to God; and the peace of God, which surpasses all understanding, will guard your hearts and minds through Christ Jesus."

God wants us to bring it all to him in prayer and lay it all out before him. You must do this and be thankful that he loves you unconditionally and is ready to guide and help you. Anxiety is a faith battle and through faith you will be set free. God uses the believer who makes a conviction to follow his Son Jesus Christ and he will do something to help you. Man, having a lack of patience, typically expects instant answers however, God's plan and therefore his response is timed to achieve the perfect answer tailor made just for you, his beloved. Your heavenly Father is similar to your earthly father in that both love you unconditionally and both are focused on your growth and well-being.

How do you get in touch with God, Jesus Christ and the Holy Spirit? First, you must realize that God has been knocking at your door and trying to get your attention. The scripture says to knock, seek and find and let your needs be known to God. It all sounds so simple to be true and it is, if you don't expect only instantaneous results. However, I personally know from my own experience and from the testimony of many others, including my Mom and Dad, that Almighty God does answer every believer's prayers.

As for my own personal testimony, I share with you that my upbringing from infancy and my exposure to the Christian church and its beliefs did have a key effect on my life and direction. However, this does not fundamentally sink in until you encounter a situation or circumstance whereby you choose to become God's disciple through your belief and acceptance of Jesus Christ as your lifetime personal Savior and you dedicate your life and direction down the path of righteousness. We can do this when we absorb the knowing that Jesus Christ as the Son of God died on the cross and was resurrected as a sacrificial act to wash away the sins of the world, including ours as well. Fortunately, this happened to me when I was seventeen. Since then I have surely not been perfect and I have strayed at times from the right track, but God has not quit loving me and he still speaks to me and he still guides me just as he always has, since his love never fails and it is forever extended to me. Knowing this is paramount since I know that without God's presence and his constant love I will no longer be able to stand tall and see the glorious light of truth that he emits. It so happens that things have come forth in my life on earth and blessings have sprung up in my midst which I view as special gifts or favors which only God could have known about or could have provided. Thanksgiving and praise are the order of the day and every day I am able to enjoy my marvelous journey on God's earth.

In a daily devotional book for April 22nd is a devotional titled "To Be Made Holy". It reads:

"Blessed is the man you discipline, O Lord,
the man you teach from your law."
Psalm 94:12

"The vinedresser is never nearer the branches
than when he is pruning them."
David Jeremiah

A Classic Devotional from Andrew Murray

Every child of God must at one time or another enter the school of trial. What the Scriptures teach us is confirmed by experience. They teach us further, that we are to count it a joy when God takes us into this school. It is part of our heavenly blessedness to be educated and sanctified by the Father through chastisement.

Holiness is the highest glory of the Father, and also of the child. He "chastens us for our profit that we may be partakers of His Holiness." In trial the Christian would often have only comfort. Or he seeks to be quiet and contented under the special chastisement. This is indeed the beginning; but the Father desires something else, something higher. He would make him holy, holy, for his whole life.

Thank You for the challenges You allow in my life to make me stronger and draw me closer to You. Amen

Remember

It's not what you accomplish in life.
It's what you overcome!

In the strong name of Jesus, the Christ!

James P. Robson

About the Author

James P. Robson was born in 1938 in Joplin, Missouri. Currently a resident of Houston, Texas, he has a professional background in accounting, finance and sales marketing. His beliefs include the principle that "thoughts are things" both individually and collectively, and that all manifestations first resided in the intangible realm of thought and faith. He believes in infinite possibilities when the mind and the heart are aligned and focused. He is the father of two sons and a daughter and has six grandchildren. He can be reached at: jamesrobson@comcast.net.

All Books Written by the Author

The Music of the Heart
The Inner Voice if the Heart
The Spirit of the Heart
The Gift of the Heart
The Mission of the Heart
The Love of the Heart
The Glory of the Heart
The Intuitive Wisdom of the Heart

Lightning Source UK Ltd.
Milton Keynes UK
UKHW010255070622
404039UK00011B/158/J

9 781947 620964